I'm Somebody and So Are You!

THE HUMAN CONNECTION IN EDUCATION

For Safer Schools and Environments

VERA RIPP HIRSCHHORN, M.S.

VRH CONSULTANTS
Creating Curricula for Social Change
A Division of America's Young Heroes Publications

Published by
America's Young Heroes Publications
BOCA RATON, FLORIDA

Copyright © 2018 by Vera Ripp Hirschhorn, M.S.

All rights reserved under International and Pan-American Copyright Conventions. Unless otherwise noted, no part of this book may be reproduced, stored in a retrieval system, or transmitted in any form or by any means, graphic, electronic, or mechanical, including photocopying, recording, taping, or otherwise, without express written permission of the author, publisher, except for brief quotations.

ISBN: 978-0-9718197-4-0

Printed in the United States of America

To purchase other books by the author, visit Amazon.com or CreatingCurriculum.com

Front cover image from original collage by Vera Ripp Hirschhorn, M.S.
Original cover photography and author bio photo by GarrinEvanStudios
Interior and cover design by Gary A. Rosenberg

Dedications

My family members, your spirits live on despite the silencing of your voices due to prejudice, hatred, bigotry, and intolerance in the 1940s:

Grandma Maria Berger Ripp and Grandpa Hinko Ripp, Grandpa Emmanuel Friebert, Aunts Irene Ripp Keller, Margita, Alzbeta, Ibola, Yolande, Munzi, Vojtech, and Irena Friebert. Young cousins Mira age 7, Elvira age 11, Ervin age 8, and Eva age 6. Ella Ripp, Jozika Ripp, Roza Ripp, and Melita Ripp.

And a special dedication to my Uncle Imre Ripp, who fought in the underground resistance movement. How I wish I could have met you all and Uncle Imre, I am so proud of you!

Mira age 7, Elvira age 11.

All righteous people and resistance fighters of exemplary character. Empathetic, open-minded, confident, optimistic role models who risked their lives to save others.

Raoul Wallenberg: I wouldn't be here today without your heroic intervention to save my parents.

In Memory of . . .

My loving, heroic, courageous, and resilient parents, Daniel Ripp and Judith Friebert Ripp: victims of genocide, victors in life. Your unconditional love inspired me to pursue my life's passion with purpose: to create curricula for teachers to empower students to promote self-respect, respect for each other's diversities, and to prevent bullying—the foundation for genocide.

In Remembrance of . . .

All the students, teachers, and others who lost their lives tragically in episodes of school violence.

In Praise of . . .

The heroic role models at Marjory Stoneman Douglas High School in Parkland, Florida, who transformed from victims into victors and triumphed over tragedy! They transformed their stories of anxieties, fears, and pain into stories of passion with a purpose for action, for their benefit and the benefit of society. They empowered, encouraged, and educated their peers—and even adults— to take action for social change and social justice.

In Honor of . . .

My loving, supportive, precious family: Martin, Genene, Garrin, Hank, Maureen, Nicole, Daren, and Deanna

I'm Somebody & So Are You!

Vera Ripp Hirschhorn

Let's revere our differences and exalt our likenesses;
Let's strive for oneness.

Let's embrace with grace,
Our imperfections and our perfections.

Let's share our fears and our pain
As they dissolve down memory lane.
And let's celebrate the victories in our histories.

Let's empathize and harmonize,
Compromise and aggrandize:
The greatness of you and the greatness of me.*

This poem was inspired by Emily Dickinson's poem "I'm Nobody! Who are you?" (1891), the exact antithesis to the underlying theme of my life's work.

*Inspired by my daughter.

"Students are like seeds in the garden of our classroom that need to be nurtured and cultivated by us, their teachers. In so doing, they can blossom into flowering plants that can bear 'fruit' of many different kinds to benefit themselves and others."

—Vera Ripp Hirschhorn

Contents

Letters to Educators, Parents, and
 Community Leaders 1

Teaching Tool I—Stress Reduction Techniques
 for Mind, Body & Spirit: 7

Teaching Tool II—Self & Peer Assessment
 for Personal Growth 23

Teaching Tool III—Storytelling to Develop
 Empathy and Compassion 35

Teaching Tool IV—"What If" Scenarios
 for Cultivating Relationships 47

Teaching Tool V—Volunteering/Mentoring
 to Pursue Passion with Purpose 55

Appendix I—Bullying Prevention Programs,
 Presentations & Proclamations 67

Appendix II—Art with Heart Projects by
 FAU Future Teachers 91

Appendix III—My Dad's Story 95

Appendix IV—My Stories 103

My Gratitude List 119

About the Author 123

Praise for *I'm Somebody and So Are You!*

"I plan to share the book with my colleagues who teach the middle grades and high school, because we are all talking about the concerns we have about increased anxieties, depression, bullying and suicides in our student populations. Recognizing genocide, such as the Holocaust, as the most extreme form of bullying is an important note as children and teens who are unable to express their identities, their passions and their fears become afflicted with diagnosed or undiagnosed conditions of anxiety and depression at alarmingly increasing rates in the U.S.

Expressive arts, mindfulness, deep breathing and positive self-talk become an essential part of a curriculum that contains the human element and this book provides teachers with the tools and the incentive to integrate the tools in their subject area curricula and address the age of alienation that young students find normal.

The link between the suggested activities and the 'soft skills' that *Forbes Magazine* described as missing from the skill set of this generation's graduates is especially useful in encouraging teachers and teacher education students to study and implement story-telling. The arts connection is equally well linked through the author's presentation of her own personal story, modeling vulnerability as a valid state of expression and sharing her pathway to teaching the whole child/person. Music, drama, puppetry, visual art, writing and volunteering may be just right for getting at 'soft skills' for students given their multiple intelligences profile, their diverse backgrounds, their learning style preferences and their prior educational experiences.

An important learning from my first attempt at utilizing some of the book's story-telling exercises in my university classes for music education students is to consider the mindfulness and breathing as preparatory components. College students who have not experienced the safe spaces, encouragement and benefits of personal artistic expression alone or in groups need the time and the assistance to set their biases and hurried schedules aside for best results.

My music education students' experiences with the 'Teachers in Training' storytelling yielded deeper responses about their own journeys, than prompts I have used previously about their decision to become educators. We have changed the assignment to incorporate this excellent and simple process to help university students formulate their self-portrait as a teacher, and understand their basis for decisions about teaching."

—Susan W. Mills, Ed.D., Professor and Director of Music Education, Hayes School of Music, Appalachian State University

U.S. Congressman Ted Deutch's congratulatory praises recorded in the 112th Congressional Records for Vera's anti-bullying campaign throughout Florida's secondary schools.

Congressional Record

United States of America
PROCEEDINGS AND DEBATES OF THE 112th CONGRESS, FIRST SESSION

Tuesday, May 31, 2011

House of Representatives

Mr. Speaker,

I rise today to recognize the twenty-six students from Florida schools that have been named winners in the America's Young Heroes contest to promote respect and prevent bullying. These students have admirably put forth concrete, practical, and creative solutions to prevent bullying in America's schools. However, even more important than the proposals is the contest's climate of acceptance and respect that is being spread to schools across Florida through the America's Young Heroes Program.

Founded by Vera Hirschhorn, the America's Young Heroes contest was created in 1999 to improve student's self-esteem through the submission of original stories, poems, music, short films, and artwork about their experiences with bullying. The America's Young Heroes contest has dedicated itself to remedying the bullying epidemic facing our schools by placing an emphasis on positive thoughts and actions to solve bullying situations.

I congratulate Vera Hirschhorn, the America's Young Heroes contest, and the twenty-six Florida students for their great work to end bullying in our schools. Their great work and advocacy on behalf of respect and acceptance is truly making Florida schools a safer place for our children.

TED DEUTCH
Member of Congress

Congressional Record

United States of America
PROCEEDINGS AND DEBATES OF THE 112th CONGRESS, FIRST SESSION

April 17, 2012

House of Representatives

HONORING the
11th Annual America's Young Heroes Contest
HON. THEODORE E. DEUTCH of Florida
in the House of Representatives

Dear Mr. Speaker,

I rise today in celebration of the 11th annual America's Young Heroes contest, which honors students who have created visual art, film, poetry and essays to promote self-empowerment and combat bullying. These students have undoubtedly fostered more tolerant communities in South Florida as well as across the country, and I applaud their efforts.

Last year in the United States, nearly 5.7 million middle school and high school students were bullied. Even more tragic is the fact that almost one in five teens who were victims of bullying contemplated ending their own lives. America's Young Heroes provides a vital platform for teens to address these problems in a way that helps promote positive change.

I congratulate the organizers and participants of the America's Young Heroes contest for operating under the shared belief that in America, no child should be afraid to go to school because he or she is experiencing bullying. It is my hope that because of their efforts, we can work towards a future where all schools are a safe place for students to learn and grow.

Ted Deutch
MEMBER OF CONGRESS

Quotes from teachers-in-training at Florida Atlantic University's College of Education:

"Vera gave us a Toolkit and a Handbook of Tools for confidence and the courage we need on how we can help our students."

"Vera was well-informed on how to address every child and help students to understand, express, and deal with their feelings and alleviate stress. Starting mindfulness techniques at an early age and learning activities that help the classroom 'go upward' were useful strategies."

"Self-reflecting is important as a future leader/teacher. Once we know who we are and how we feel, then, we can better our future and the world. I must be a role model so that students may follow my positive examples."

"I will be more cognizant and accepting of the differences of all individuals. I will encourage respect among students, their peers and communities and for them to be true to themselves and not conform . . . you can be an individual and still belong."

"I learned a creative way to introduce the importance and excitement of diversity. I also learned to respect and appreciate the stories of others."

"The project has shown how important it is to be flexible and the benefits of stepping out of our comfort zone."

"One project showed how we can make ourselves feel more comfortable around each other, and get to know our peers and students."

"It helped us find similarities with others and appreciate differences."

"I truly believe in your philosophy and know that your curriculum has value for students and teachers. The future of education depends upon teaching and learning that focuses on caring and trusting relationships. The key to learning is to value others and yourself."
—Dr. Susannah Brown, Professor of Art Education, Florida Atlantic University

"I feel your teaching tools are perfect. I'm a big fan of storytelling because I believe that's how you engage heart and you mentioned how that's tied with developing empathy and compassion. The scenarios are very valuable based on how you laid them out; the research is clear that you need an action plan to know how to act in certain situations before you're actually in them. Teaching Tool IV really helps with that. I love Teaching Tool V. When you take your eyes off yourself and put them on other people, you don't struggle as much with problems. You're caught up with something bigger than yourself. I really like your book and hope you continue to get it into schools. I'm glad you took the time to write this. I also love how you honored your family and that's incredibly important. Let me know what I can do to help and support you as you continue to carry the torch when it comes to these issues."
—Dr. Sameer Hinduja, Ph.D., Professor, School of Criminology and Criminal Justice; Cyber-Bullying Research Center, Florida Atlantic University

"What a wonderful publication! This book is going to be easily applied in the classroom and beyond— even in home-school environments. Bravo!"
—Heather

Letter to Educators, Parents, and Community Leaders

The following excerpts from my beloved Dad's story are about his life of survival in a world devastated by prejudice, hatred and fear. As a child, I grew up hearing my Dad's nightly nightmares and was consumed in his painful stories of the tragic loss of all my grandparents, aunts, uncles and four young cousins whose only crime was their religion:

> "We had to sleep in the woods under all weather conditions; our clothes and shoes began to disintegrate to the point that they no longer had soles on them. We were always hungry. We managed to find dirty potatoes and drank green polluted rainwater and developed dysentery. I ran a fever for days and was skin and bones and was so weak that I would fall each time I tried to stand up. But *I never gave up hope of seeing my Mother once again.* Also, God gave me strength.
>
> We had to continue to put mines in the roads, deeper and deeper. We began to freeze and I remembered my Dad's survival stories when he served in WWI. So, I began to constantly rub my face, hands, feet and all body parts to keep the blood circulating and prevent frostbite. I taught the others to do the same and we managed to survive.

Sometimes, they would begin shooting at random and kill some of the men. Once, I whispered to the survivors to lie down and pretend they were dead if and when the shooting would begin again."

As an educator, I transformed my painful feelings into my purpose of implementing character and civics education. Given my family's tragic background with genocide, I wanted to help transform bullies into benevolent beings and victims into victors because I believe that bullying is the foundation for genocide. Thus, I created the Spirit of Heroes arts program for teaching tolerance and understanding as well as the America's Young Heroes anti-bullying program and contest[1] for safe schools and safe environments. Students' solutions were expressed via essays, poetry, visual and performing arts, songs and/or short films.

Now, more than ever, in this technological age of cyber bullying, isolation, alienation, and school violence, I want to continue to help educators and students, of today and tomorrow, develop social skills and learn how to solve social problems via the *power of the arts*. I want them to feel empowered and feel better about themselves; I want to help them get to know who they are and find meaning and purpose in their life for their betterment and the betterment of others.

I'm Somebody & So Are You! The Human Connection in Education for Safer Schools & Environments: A Toolkit for Encouraging Personal Growth is intended to assist teachers and motivate students to:

1. nurture mind, body and spirit in order to prevent emotional and physical burn-out; (*Tool I—Stress-reduction techniques*)

2. discover and explore their weakness and strengths, their uniqueness, talents, passions and character attributes via activities for personal growth; (*Tool II—Self & Peer Assessment*)

3. share stories in order to *develop* more empathy and acceptance of each other's feelings and imperfections; *(Tool III—Storytelling)*

4. generate "soft skills"[2] and cultivate personal and interpersonal relationships, communication, teamwork and problem-solving skills; and serve as role models to prevent bullying and promote self-respect and respect for each other's differences while finding common ground. *(Tool IV—"What If" Scenarios)*

5. envision and act upon a passion with purpose to benefit themselves and others. *(Tool V—Volunteering/Mentoring)*

We have all witnessed at home, school or community the rise in bullying/cyber bullying, a contributing factor to students' depression, anxiety, rage, revenge, suicide, and/or school violence.[3] Mental health professionals have acknowledged this increase; students themselves have asked for help.[4] Everyone wants to feel safe, loved and respected. The Columbine perpetrators, who were bullied and became bullies themselves, expressed their need for respect. In fact, in 1999, they stated in a video a week before the tragic shootings, "maybe next week we'll get the respect we deserve." In writings, the mother of Adam Lanza, the shooter at Newtown's Sandy Hook Elementary, lamented that "her son's isolation will likely get worse, in part because of poor relationships developed at school."[5] Nicholas Cruz, the shooter of Parkland's Marjory Stoneman Douglas High School said in 2019, "Maybe I should get the death penalty. I just want love."[6]

With the public health approach to school violence, researcher Ron Avi Astor at the University of Southern California and others believe that prevention instead of reacting is the key; that is, "if you devote resources to shutting down bullying, discrimination and harassment, there is a chance to de-escalate conflict before it starts."[7]

"What if" we immersed our students in daily or weekly **teaching tools** that taught them to practice deep breathing exercises, positive self-talk and gratitude journaling? "What if" they participated in self and peer assessment exercises or engaged in interrelation skills as in role-playing, problem solving and other forms of soft skills? "What if" students learned compassion and respect by listening to the stories of sadness, fears or anger of their peers and then told their own stories? "What if" they found meaning in their life by volunteering/mentoring to help one another. "What if" students became more aware of their human-ness?

These teaching tools were tested with future teachers at Florida Atlantic University in Boca Raton, Florida, thanks to Dr. Susannah Brown, their professor. Dr. Brown and I both received verbal and written positive feedback from them. Also, at the beginning of the semester, there were no visible relationships; at the end, there were those of mutual respect, camaraderie and shared creativity within each team of three, four or five teachers-in-training.

One teacher-in-training said, "I became more aware of different strategies I could use in the classroom to help students relax and release tension so that they could focus on assignments." Another added, "upon self-reflecting, I must be a **role model** so that students can follow my positive examples." Another would-be teacher stated, "What if" scenarios would greatly teach students how to constructively solve a problem with others and how to positively change their mindset."

I have observed how students changed perspectives and thus changed their lives and the lives of others through the *power of the arts*. Teachers-in training learned the importance of getting to know themselves first before taking steps in the process of impacting change for the better. Their art projects and exhibits[8] such as "Art has Character," the Heart to Heart Collages or their Inner/Outer Boxes as well as their colorful ceramic pieces displayed detailed self-representation; they also demonstrated their sense of professional responsibility to create and affect positive change for themselves, their students and their peers on campus.

I'm Somebody & So Are You! The Human Connection in Education for Safer Schools & Environments: A Toolkit for Encouraging Personal Growth blossomed by listening to my Dad's Story[9] and his experiences with genocide and from telling my own story[10] with its highs and lows of my life's journey. Upon telling my story and why and how I found meaning in my life to Dr. Susannah Brown's College of Education students, they began to share theirs. It is my wish that these stories serve as inspirational "seeds" to tell your own personal story of self-revelation and self-exploration; and in turn encourage your students to share their story, exploring who they are, why they are here and how they will find meaning in their life for the betterment of self and others.

1. Appendix I: Teaching Tolerance & Anti-Bullying contests, Florida's Schools; Blogs with Students' Solutions via the Arts; Proclamations for America's Young Heroes Month- Mayor of Boca Raton; Superintendent and the School Board of the School District of Palm Beach County; Board of County Commissioners of Palm Beach County, Florida

2. *Forbes Magazine,* May 17, 2016, "These Are the Skills Bosses Say New College Grads Do Not Have," Karsten Strauss

3. *Sun-Sentinel,* April 22, 2019, Emily Swanson, Carolyn Thompson, Hannah Fingerhut, "Poll: Parents worry about how safe schools are." The Associate Press-NORC poll of 1,063 adults was conducted March 14–18, 2019 using a sample drawn from NORC's probability-based AmeriSpeak Panel

   Psychology Today, March 2018, George S. Every, Jr., Ph.D., "Profiling" School Shooters

   ABC News, February 22, 2018, Emily Shapiro, Lauren Effron, Margaret Dawson, Christina Ng, Tess Scott, "Dissecting the Distinctive Profile of School Shooters: There's Always a Trail of What They're About to Do"

4. *Time Magazine,* November 7, 2016, Schrobsdorff "Teen Depression & Anxiety: Why the Kids Are Not Alright!"

   Time Magazine, April 9, 2018, Katie Reilly "Depression on Campus"

5. *Hartford Courant,* December 9, 2018, Josh Kovner and Dave Altimari

6. *New York Times,* April 11, 2019, Patricia Mazzei "Parkland Families, Citing Negligence, File Suits"

7. NprED *How Learning Happens,* March 7, 2018, Anya Kamenetz, "Here's How to Prevent the Next School Shooting, Experts Say"

8. Appendix II—FAU's College of Education, Images by teachers in training of art projects and exhibits on Self Reflection and on their Journey for Personal and Professional Development

9. Appendix III—My Dad's Interview with his grandson and Questions to Think About

10. Appendix IV—Excerpt from the Introduction to *Childhood,* Chapter I from my poetic memoir, *The Circle of Life: My Story*

TEACHING TOOL 1—
Stress Reduction Techniques for Mind, Body & Spirit:
Deep Breathing, Mindfulness, Positive Self-Talk, Gratitude Journaling, and Healthy Eating

"The bell of mindfulness tolls in each moment, inviting us to come to our senses, reminding us that we can wake up to our lives, now, while we have them to live.... Only that day dawns to which we are awake."
—Henry David Thoreau (*WALDEN*)

Students of all ages and grade levels can benefit from deep breathing exercises, mindfulness, positive self-talk, gratitude journaling, healthy dietary habits, and creative expression through the arts. In an article, "The Kids Are Not All Right," from the  November 2016 issue of *Time Magazine*, reference was made to a teen who healed gradually by practicing deep breathing exercises, positive self-talk, and channeling feelings of anxiety, depression, and self-harm into creating a film. She wrote and directed it with about thirty kids. The film project became a teaching tool.

According to Ellen Chance, co-president of the Palm Beach School Counselor Association, anxiety and depression have affected kids as early as the fifth grade. This is due to school pressures, technology, relationships, and online bullying.

Congressman Tim Ryan who was immersed in one of Dr. Jon Kabat-Zinn's[1] mindfulness retreats has been so excited about his calming, productive experiences in his everyday life that he has written a book about it. He has even obtained a million dollars of federal funds to teach it to school children in his Ohio district because he has "seen it transform classrooms . . . and . . . what it does to individuals who have really high chronic levels of stress and how it has helped their body heal itself."

On October 24, 2015, the *New York Times* printed an article entitled, "City Classrooms Give Pupils a Moment to Turn Inward." It reported on how delighted the Chancellor, Carmen Farina, of New York City schools was at seeing a "hushed room full of fourth-grade children sitting cross-legged on the floor as they were guided by one of their peers." The fourth grade guide asked students to "please let your eyes close and take three mindful breaths" while he gently struck a

---

1. Dr. Jon Kabat-Zinn is Professor of Medicine Emeritus and creator of the Stress Reduction Clinic and the Center for Mindfulness in Medicine, Health Care, and Society at the University of Massachusetts Medical School.

"Mindfulness is awareness that arises through paying attention, on purpose, in the present moment, non-judgmentally," says Dr. Kabat-Zinn.

shallow bronze bowl and produced a *gong* sound. This bowl can be replaced with a bell, a flute, or any other instrument, as well as sounds of nature. In a diverse class, instruments of different sounds and cultures can also be used.

One student in a Los Angeles classroom said that practicing mindfulness "makes me want to come to school." Another student said that "it makes me more happy within myself and, I guess, more patient with others."

A third student confessed that "when I'm in a better mood, my family's in a better mood" and "I don't argue as much with my sister . . . nothing bugs me."

According to their principal, Jennifer Garcia, "Their school," like forty-three others who have adopted the program, "has changed for the better. Kids are calm and they're not taking stuff out on each other." Garcia added, "They're really engaged in wanting to be helpful with each other."

On December 2, 2015, the *Sun Sentinel* reported on the Geekiwood 2015 conference for middle and high school girls that included mindfulness exercises, at Florida International University in Miami.

---

2. Goebel credits mindfulness for saving her life after surviving a terrible car accident and for helping her graduate from Florida Atlantic University with honors, as well as finding success in the tech fields:

> "As a woman who was in technology, it was important to remain focused, confident, efficient, and be an excellent problem-solver with sharp business intuition," Goebel stated. "Mindfulness helped me do all of that in a male-dominated industry."

Goebel has quit the tech field to become a full-time mindfulness instructor for corporations.

As a result, Michelle Goebel,[2] "a technology whiz" from Boca Raton, Florida, encouraged over 200 girls to succeed in STEM programs through the practice of mindfulness.

Dr. Susannah Brown, Associate Professor of Art at the College of Education, Florida Atlantic University, and I tested these stress reduction tools with her future teachers.

Feedback from Teachers-in-Training

> "[The tools] helped me be aware of different strategies I could use in the classroom to help students relax and release tension so that they could focus on assignments."

> "These sessions actually led me to do breathing exercises with my students to help with calming them down. Deep breathing is definitely a part of my life now and I will keep it there."

> "The sessions influenced me to allow future students to keep a journal of feelings."

> "I also enjoyed learning new techniques like deep breathing and mindfulness. These tips and tricks can be applied in the classroom to make a better learning environment."

> "I learned 'to express who I am as a person and to show what's important.'"

> "The three sessions [of teaching tools] showed me how to relax and take my time."

> "The human interaction [in teams], reviewing what we went over in previous discussions, and the breathing exercises that made me relax [influenced me]."

Teaching Tool I—Stress Reduction Techniques for Mind, Body & Spirit

Thanks to the work of Dr. Albert Ellis on Rational Emotional Behavior Techniques and his REBT Self-Help Form, students have learned the transformative power of **positive-self talk** from victim-type feelings of suffering and helplessness to a victor-type feeling of hope when faced with challenges.

Below is a brief outline of the process:

A. For awareness:

One can acknowledge, "I am aware of the problem" (internal, external, real or imagined; past, present, or future)

B. For identification of one's Negative Beliefs, one might look at signs such as:

   a. Self-made demands on oneself and others (I/he *must* or *should*)

   b. Awfulizing (It's awful, horrible, terrible)

   c. Judgments of self or others (I/he/she is bad, worthless)

   d. Low Frustration Tolerance (I can't stand it)

C. For choosing to transform negative beliefs into positive beliefs:

   a. Examples of daily positive self-talk include:
   - I prefer, I wish, I desire rather than I demand
   - I realize that the situation is unfortunate and bad
   - I realize that I don't like it but I can stand it and handle it

Benefits of Dr. Ellis's work in cognitive behavioral techniques include the replacement of destructive, unhealthy negative emotions such as rage, anxiety, shame, hurt, jealousy, guilt, embarrassment, and depression with *new healthy negative emotions and expressions* such as:

- Disappointment (I am disappointed)
- Concern (I am concerned)
- Annoyance (I am annoyed)
- Sadness (I am sad)
- Regret (I regret)
- Frustration (I am frustrated)

One of Dr. Brown's College of Education students wrote:

> "Encouraging 'positive self-talk' in the classroom is wonderful because it encourages all students to look at themselves and their whole lives in a positive way."

STRESS REDUCTION ACTIVITIES

1. Teachers ask and remind students to be mindful of how they enter into a classroom, sit down, and nonjudgmentally observe details of their surroundings . . . the walls, books, etc., while they wait for the teacher to begin the lesson.[3]

2. Five minutes of deep breathing exercises can be implemented at the beginning of each class to calm students so that they can be better focused for the lesson.

3. Positive self-talk can be taught and practiced during challenging "What If" scenarios to help transform victim-type feelings of helplessness to victor-type feelings of hopefulness.

4. Students can design and create their personal "gratitude journals" that can be collected and put in a safe place under lock and key.

---

3. See the example for a mindfulness and visualization exercise on page 30.

Teaching Tool I—Stress Reduction Techniques for Mind, Body & Spirit

5. Each day or the beginning and end of each week, students express their gratitude for the good and bad in their daily life through poetry, art, collage, photos, etc.

6. Julia Cameron, author of *The Artist's Way*, has helped students unleash their creativity by suggesting that they practice *stream of consciousness journaling*, that is, writing three nonstop, unedited, nonjudgmental *breakfast pages* each day. I've also used this format and found it to be most valuable with benefits of increased clarification, insights, and even resolution for uncomfortable, painful situations.

7. All journals can be handmade and embellished with sketches, drawings, letters, poems, lists, ticket stubs, and quotes. They can be used by students at the beginning of all interdisciplinary classes.

8. Author Stephanie Dowrick has offered detailed techniques, exercises, and *themes* for free expression of thoughts and feelings for theme-based journals.[4] Such journals are the foundation for art projects such as collages, which students at all levels can create, as did future teachers at Florida Atlantic University's College of Education classes, taught by Dr. Susannah Brown and myself. Dr. Brown suggests that the teacher should preface gratitude journaling or any other form of journals by deciding whether

---

4. Such themes include:

"The gifts that I can offer the world include . . ." "The best way I know to get over disappointment is . . ."

"A letter to someone I hurt;" "A letter to someone who hurt me;" "Tough times have taught me that . . ."

"What nature has taught me is . . ." "I am most proud of when . . ."

"I have the power to . . ." "My way of expressing compassion is . . ." "The most positive way I express my pain is . . ."

or not it's for a student's own personal use or not. That is, is it intended for reading and sharing or not? Also, journals can just include symbols to reflect items of gratitude depending on the grade or ability of students.

9. Mind and body are interconnected. How and what we think affects the health of our body and vice versa. How and what we eat affects our mind. Organic foods, preferably plant-based with high fiber and without the pesticides are richer in nutrients than the packaged, highly processed sugar and high fat foods; the latter are deficient in vitamins, minerals and amino acids that are so necessary for our mental, emotional and physical well-being. Organic turkey, chicken and wild salmon with unprocessed carbohydrates and produce are equally more nourishing than non-organic.

A team of students can choose to research the effects of the deficiency of a nutrient. As an example, one student could research the B Complex vitamins, especially B6, important for our moods; another could research and even speak to health professionals on the deficiency of different types of minerals such as zinc; another could interview a nutritionist on the effects of amino acid deficiencies. Another team member could research certain familial genetic dispositions such as the MTHFR gene mutation; this is the inability to utilize specific B Vitamins necessary for healthy neurotransmission. The student could investigate healthy remedies such as methylfolate, a nutritional supplement. Without it, the deficiency could lead to depression, anxiety and processing disorders.

Please note: A "relaxation" section of the classroom can include art and craft supplies for the design and creation of gratitude journals, graphic instructions for different kinds of breathing exercises, and graphic instructions for positive self-talk exercises.

Teaching Tool I—Stress Reduction Techniques for Mind, Body & Spirit

Validation for Stress Reduction Techniques

Dr. Jon Kabat-Zinn, PhD, has demonstrated the transformative effects of mindfulness on our mental, emotional, and physical health. He has also shown its usefulness for anxiety, depression, and pain as well as improvements in memory and attention.

Students studying to be physicians, nurses and counselors at the University of Minnesota have been learning how to care for their patients and themselves through nutritious meals and mindful eating habits. "And because burnout and stress are common among health care providers, they have learned how to eat mindfully, taking deep breaths before eating, sitting down to dine with others and slowing down enough to taste their food. They have also kept a journal and recorded their eating habits."[5]

These future health professionals have been participating in a course entitled Food Matters for Health Professionals which pairs the art of cooking with the science of using food as medicine. They have joined other students in ten medical schools in the field of culinary medicine to focus on prevention rather than treatment.

Under the direction of Dr. Kate Shafto, assistant professor at the University of Minnesota's medical school and chef Jenny Breen, students formed teams and received case studies of fictional patients as if they were struggling with a variety of diseases. Each team needed to create a main dish to help their patient.

One student, studying counseling psychology and his team chose a Korean dish with kimchi containing fermented vegetables. His team decided on this recipe because they learned that fermented foods

---

5. *Sun-Sentinel*, February 4, 2018, "From meal plan to heal plan" & *Minneapolis Star Tribune* by Allie Shah

can improve gut health and help with anxiety and depression, due to many neurotransmitters in the gut.

Dr. James W. Pennebaker, author of *Writing to Heal*, at the University of Texas in Austin, has assigned students the exercise of "writing down their deepest feelings about an emotional upheaval in their life for fifteen or twenty minutes a day for four consecutive days. Many found their immune systems strengthened. Others saw their grades improved. Sometimes entire lives have changed."

Politicians and employees at some of the top workplaces, such as Google and Apple, have used tools of mindfulness. In fact, mindfulness for corporate employees has gained much appeal. An article in the March 12, 2017, edition of the *Sun-Sentinel* newspaper stated that "large companies are becoming more aware of the role that mental health could and should play in their corporate wellness programs."

Dr. John Denniger, director of research at the Benson-Henry Institute for Mind Body Medicine in Boston, Massachusetts, indicated that mindfulness can help one lose weight, lower blood pressure, ease irritable bowel syndrome, sleep better, and quit smoking.

According to Dr. Denniger, mindfulness, in some studies, has demonstrated an impact at the cellular level, slowing down the effects of aging and increasing neuroplasticity, which is the ability of the brain to grow new brain cells and develop new connections. Dr. Denniger began practicing mindfulness in 1973, twice a day.

Breathing exercises such as alternate nostril breathing have been shown to help control blood pressure, improve heart rate, make arteries more flexible, and activate the parasympathetic nervous system, which calms down the body's fight or flight adrenal response to stress. Dr. Luciano Bernardi, an internal medicine

Teaching Tool I—Stress Reduction Techniques for Mind, Body & Spirit

professor of the University of Pavia, Italy, did research that shows the benefits of slow breathing exercises; he found that they improve exercise capacity in patients with chronic heart failure. Also, "slow breathing activates areas in the brain connected with anti-depressive activities."

Dr. Andrew Weil, M.D., founder of the Arizona Center for Integrative Medicine at the University of Arizona, added, "I think breath is the only function through which you can influence the involuntary nervous system."

As a woman who has juggled the roles of daughter, spouse, parent, and educator, the practice of *deep breathing* and *mindfulness* of fragrances, aromas, textures, and/or sights while walking in the park, cooking, eating, or washing my dishes, or even my hair, have kept me grounded and balanced. *Positive self-talk and gratitude journaling* have elevated my moods and resulted in happier relationships. *Gratitude journaling*, popularized by Sarah Ban Breathnach, helped me realize that even challenging people or situations are "blessings or gifts in disguise" and offer us an opportunity for personal growth. One of my "gifts" was to learn to express compassion and empathy with boundaries. Writing about emotional experiences can have positive health benefits.

In summary, if we want to feel better about ourselves and others, we need to practice being mindful of our thoughts, words, and responses to challenging people and/or situations. We have the power to practice an *attitude of gratitude* for the good and bad in our daily lives, realizing that they're "gifts" to strengthen us in our personal growth. We have the power to be mindful of the stories we tell ourselves and others . . . stories that can transform our negative, unhealthy expressions of feelings to more positive and healthier ones for ourselves and others at home and in the school, community, and workforce.

> *"In life there are storms.*
> *We must remember to play after every storm;*
> *and celebrate the gift of life as we have it, or else*
> *life becomes a task, rather than a gift.*
> *We must always listen to the songs in our heart,*
> *and share that song with others."*
> —From **HEART SONG** by Mattie Stepanek
> (died at age 13 on June 22, 2004, from muscular dystrophy)

Example of a Mindfulness and Visualization Exercise with Teachers and Students, at the Beginning of a Lesson

Imagine yourself at the ocean, just before sunrise;
And as you hear the peaceful sounds of the waves, come in and out,
Breathe in relaxation and peace
And breathe out tension and tight muscles.

Once again, breathe in acceptance
And breathe out resistance.

Again, as you hear the gentle sounds of the waves, come in and out,
Breathe in positivity
And breathe out negativity.

Now imagine yourself feeling the light from the rising of the sun;
Feel it shine its soothing light on the top of your head.
Feel it flow down to your eyes, relaxing them with healthy
    sight and insights.
Feel it soothe your throat, your heart with feelings of love,
    empathy, and compassion.
Feel it flow down to your belly, calming and empowering it gently.
Feel the light relax your sacrum
And lastly, your tailbone.

Soon, your inner voice asks you,
What joy will I give myself today?
What joy will I give to another?
What joy will I receive from another?

As the balmy breezes begin to bring you back to the present moment, YOU STAND, REFRESHED, REVITALIZED, READY TO START A BRAND-NEW DAY.

Post Stress-Reduction Exercise

Q. So, how do you feel?

Q. Do you feel that this benefitted you? Do you feel that you would consider incorporating this exercise into your lesson plans to benefit you and your students?

The visualization at the ocean is a form of Storytelling as per **Teaching Tool III.**

Teaching Tool I includes stress reduction exercises such as:

1. Deep breathing,

2. Mindfulness with sensory images to relax the mind and body,

3. Gratitude and stream of consciousness journaling, and

4. Positive self-talk techniques.

The entire relaxation process helps set an intention to have, give and receive joy. Self-reflecting on the following questions is from **Teaching Tool II** in Self & Peer Assessment.

1. What joy will I give myself?

2. What joy will I give to another?

3. What joy will I receive from another?

It also asks students to stand up, feel refreshed and revitalized to start a brand-new day. This is intended to inspire and empower students with confidence in resolving or dealing, calmly, with unforeseen challenges. Also, it can, possibly, help prepare students for Volunteering/Mentoring (**Teaching Tool V**), and/or "What If" Scenarios (**Teaching Tool IV**).

Who Am I?"
(Why am I here? What's my purpose?)
Vera Ripp Hirschhorn

I am the one who is nourished with the colorful **palette**
    of music, poetry and dance;
I am the one who thrives on love like the inseparable **mallard**,
    its mate and family.
Or the monarch attracted to milkweed and transforms from
    caterpillar to **butterfly**.
Like the hummingbird, nurtured by the sweet nectar of lilies
    and **lupines**.

I am the one who is grateful to **flora and fauna** like the turtle,
    Who's taught me to slow down.

I am the one who lives life with passion and purpose:

Celebrating victorious parents of genocide
And Teens who are Heroes, too!
Telling their story of triumph over tragedy
Unlike my four young cousins who perished, due to hatred
    and bigotry.

I am the one who gave a VOICE to Teens
To prevent bullying and promote respect through the Arts.

I am the one who believes in New Beginnings
I am the one for Change!

This poem was inspired by my original collage, created at my NLAPW Poetry and Collage Workshop for members and guests in 2016 (see the following page).

TEACHING TOOL II—
Self & Peer Assessment

*"O the joy of that vast elemental sympathy
which only the human soul is capable of generating
and emitting in steady and limitless floods"*
—WALT WHITMAN

Using Selfies for self-assessment in this tech age can be a fun introduction into the topic of exploring and discovering oneself.

Ask students to reflect on the following:

- Who Am I?

- Why am I here?

- How can I find meaning in my life and live with purpose for my benefit and the benefit of others?

Students can also research the historical origins for the art of selfies and study the artists who have created their own self portraits before the selfie from Albrecht Durer to Rembrandt and from Claude Monet, Pablo Picasso, Frida Kahlo, Andy Warhol through today.

Students can research and interview parents to discover more about their childhood from infancy and beyond.

Grandparents can be interviewed about the family's genealogy, heritage, traditions and ancestors

Storytelling, stress reduction techniques, stream of consciousness, and/or gratitude journaling can lead to self-reflection and serve as a form of self-assessment. Self-assessment can lead to the awareness of choice and thus, self-empowerment.

SELF & PEER ASSESSMENT ACTIVITIES

A self-assessment questionnaire* such as the one below is also a valuable activity for potential personal and interpersonal growth for teachers and students alike:

1. What joy will I give myself today? What joy will I give another? It's my choice.

2. How have I contributed my "uniqueness," my talents/skills/interests/hobbies, and my passions to the classroom discussion(s), project(s), assignment(s), and/or community?

    a. How have I embraced my perfect imperfections, that is, my weaknesses as well as my strengths?

3. With awareness of feelings, how have I expressed acceptance, empathy, and compassion/caring for myself and someone else today?

4. Have I identified my passion? How can I share it for my benefit and/or the benefit of others?

5. With awareness and acceptance, how have I resolved some underlying issues of anger or fear of rejection or fear of criticism with positive thoughts and positive action?

*See footnote on page 37

a. What's better for me? To be angry or forgiving? To love myself or fear the opinions of others? It's my choice.

6. Did I contribute to harmony or disharmony in my interactions with peers or others?

7. Did I contribute to inclusiveness or exclusiveness? How?

8. Do I listen and wait until it's my turn to talk?

9. Have I become aware of my needs for relaxation when stressed, and practiced techniques by myself or with others to help release tension in a healthy way? (breathing techniques, mindfulness, exercise)

The following peer assessment questionnaire* can help teachers and students become more aware of the positive attributes of classmates:

1. _____ gave joy to another or showed kindness to another.

---

*The self assessment and peer assessment questionnaires are based on some of the "hero or 'assessment' activities" in *Teens Are Heroes, Too! Challenges, Choices & Character:*
- My Uniqueness (What are your positive qualities? What positive qualities do others see in you?)
- My Hero Checklist
- Talents/Skills Survey & Hobbies/Interests Survey
- Peer Identification Questionnaire
- My Learning Style Survey
- My feelings
- Creating Business Cards that reflect passions, dreams, and visions of a future career

2. _____ contributed his/her talents/skills to discussions, projects, community.

3. _____ displayed empathy, compassion.

4. _____ triumphed over adversity with positive action/behavior.

5. _____ seemed to contribute to harmony.

6. _____ led the classroom in relaxation, stress reduction exercises.

Such assessment activities can help students:

1. Identify their innate heroic attributes.

2. Identify their unique mental, emotional, physical, and spiritual intelligences, such as the discovery of one's meaning in life.

3. Increase
   - Self-awareness and positive self-expression of feelings and emotions.
   - Compassion/caring, empathy for self and others.
   - An attitude of gratitude.
   - Self-empowerment.
   - Respect for oneself and others.

Teaching Tool II—Self & Peer Assessment

The VICTOR 👍 or VICTIM 👎 quiz below is another example of *self-assessment*:

1. Am I always part of the solution or part of the problem?
2. Do I see a solution for every problem or see a problem for every solution?
3. Do I say that it may be difficult and possible or that it's possible but too difficult?
4. When I make a mistake, do I say that I was wrong and apologize or do I say that it wasn't my fault?
5. Do I say that I'm responsible for my choices or blame others for the consequences of my choices or mistakes?

Feedback for the Victor or Victim quiz from future teachers at Florida Atlantic University includes:

1. For question 4, when I make a mistake, do I say I was wrong and apologize?

    "Making a mistake and learning from it and owning up to your mistakes is a good thing because it gives you an opportunity to become a better person. It's forward learning."

2. For Question 5, do I say that I'm responsible for my choices or blame others for the consequences?

    "Being responsible for your choices means you are responsible for your happiness! Great thing!"

    "Knowing you're responsible for your happiness means you have the freedom to live whatever life you would like to create, apart from the thoughts and opinions of other people so that they have no effect on your happiness."

3. I think good self-assessment tests should include:
   - "Am I always part of the solution?"
   - "Can I trust myself to approach all situations in a positive manner?"
   - "Can I always find something positive in every situation?"
   - "Is anything ever too difficult for me? Or can I try my best at everything and be happy and grateful for the outcome because I did my best?"

Ideas for Implementation of Self & Peer Assessment Activities

1. Students can create an essay, poem, graphics, or compose stories using musical instruments, dance, song, or video on any sentiments that arise from their self or peer assessment tools. (Teachers can guide them via brainstorming sessions.)

2. Assessment activities can serve as templates for teachers in order to help them create their own self & peer assessment questions. Self-assessment questionnaires can be administered at the beginning of the school year or semester in a "Getting to Know You" format. Additionally, they can be useful at the end of each semester with or without the standard report card if the latter doesn't include such attitudinal or character assessments.

   (Comparisons of self or peer questionnaires once or more a year can help students realize that they have the power to feel better. This can also be an aide for teacher accountability.)

3. Teachers can rely on self & peer assessments to assist students in applying their talents and skills to pursue their identified

passion; additionally, teachers can encourage the pursuit of their "passion with purpose" for the betterment of self and others to help resolve social issues in schools and in the community. Such tools can help some students reflect on a higher purpose or meaning in life.

4. Art projects such as the Inner/Outer Art Boxes created by FAU teachers-in training helped them with self-representation and self-assessment. Reflecting on their feelings, interests, strengths and passions, they decorated meaningful symbols for expression.

One student decorated an outer box with different textures of earthy green and brown striped fabric and Inside a miniature diorama of the redwood forest to represent her place of solace and peace for soothing her occasional anxiety (see below). Another created the butterfly box; the outer box had meaningful, educational quotes and on the inside were empathetic messages from her young students to support and uplift her during the loss of a beloved relative.

Please Note: A section in the classroom can be devoted to copies of self & peer assessment questionnaires and surveys. Students can photograph any additional copies on their cell phones and print them at home or in the library, if desired.

Validation for Self & Peer Assessment

In my view, self & peer assessment are examples of emotional-social I.Q. or character I.Q. E.Q. is a greater predictor of personal happiness, healthier relationships and success at work than high academic I.Q. Examples of these non-cognitive or "soft" skills are empathy, compassion, restraint, persistence, communication, teamwork, problem-solving skills and leadership.

In self-assessment, a student's progress in these soft skills can be evaluated by weekly or monthly check-ups via questionnaires equivalent to those of physical check-ups as recommended by health practitioners.

Psychology scientists and professors such as Dr. John Mayer at the University of New Hampshire and Dr. Peter Salovey at Yale University realized in the 1980's that the E.Q. affected problem-solving and job satisfaction. Dr. Maurice Elias, psychology professor at Rutgers University and Director of the Rutgers Social, Emotional Learning Lab stated that "emotional literacy is the missing piece" in American education. Principal Billy Aydlett at Leataata Floyd Elementary School in Sacramento discovered that youngsters weren't progressing in academics until they got help with their social and emotional issues.

Social psychologists validate self-assessment as a valuable tool to help students become aware of a habit or behavior that seems to be

Teaching Tool II—Self & Peer Assessment

"getting in the way" of their progress at home, school, or community. The student can change that habit or behavior with questions such as:

Why am I saying or doing this? or It'll be great to discover or learn that . . .

To affect change, a student must become conscious of what motivates his/her actions. If for example, the habit or behavior deals with procrastination, Heidi Grant Halvorson, a social psychologist, suggests *a self-assessment* strategy that asks three questions:

1. Am I putting this off because I'm afraid of failure due to criticism?

2. Am I procrastinating because it's unpleasant?

3. Am I delaying this because I just don't feel like doing it?

Perhaps, a student can reframe or change his/her perception or perspective, that is, figure out ways in which the project or task can be enjoyable and make it a "want to" rather than a "have to."

Validation for self-assessment can be found in companies where employees are given questionnaires to rate their work in percentiles of "What was done?" "How it was done?" and "Accountability/Objectives" as well as "Results Achieved." Furthermore, employees have been provided and asked to give a "Description of Performance" using lists of "descriptive words to articulate positive or negative performance." A summary of  an employee's character strengths and an employee's desires and goals in the "Growth Areas" are also requested.

Thus, the use of self & peer assessment tools in schools can also assist students in preparation for the "real world" when seeking employment during their school years or upon graduation.

In teams of four or five students, I student-tested several self-assessment teaching activities such as "My Uniqueness" with future teachers at Florida Atlantic University, Boca Raton; the following are some of their reflections:

> "(The teaching tool that) helped me change was the self-evaluation tool; this allows you to really dig deep down and see who you truly are and what's important to you and why you have a passion for the things you do."

> "Self-reflecting is important as a future leader/teacher. Once we know who we are and how we feel, then we can better our future and the world. I must be a role model so that students may follow my positive examples."

> "It has influenced my being accepting of who my students are."

It was interesting to observe the personal, interpersonal, and character I.Q. growth of future teachers during the process of student-testing my self-assessment tools in teams. At the beginning of the semester Dr. Brown, their professor, and I noted that there were no visible relationships among students; at the end of the semester, we witnessed relationships of mutual respect, camaraderie, and shared creativity within each team. This was probably due to "teamwork" as well as the assigned art project and exhibit entitled, Connecting Heart-to-Heart Stories: "The Human Connection" (see photo on facing page).

Teaching Tool II—Self & Peer Assessment

This type of indirect "peer assessment" can be an asset to teacher accountability. In a previous class of future teachers, Dr. Brown and I had assigned another art project that encouraged future teachers to create an art exhibit entitled, Art Has Character: Images of How Visual Art Supports Positive Interaction for the Betterment of Others. We noticed a similar personal, interpersonal, and character I.Q. growth among students in teams. The process that led to the exhibit was most valuable to them.

Feedback from Teachers-in-Training

> "I will be more cognizant and accepting of the differences of all individuals. I will encourage respect among students, their peers, and communities and for them to be true to themselves and not conform . . . you can be an individual and still belong."

> "The project has shown how important it is to be flexible and the benefits of stepping out of our comfort zone."

"The project showed how we can make us feel more comfortable around each other."

"It helped us find similarities with others and appreciate differences."

"It allowed us 'to be creative individually and then creative together.'"

"Activities will help teach students to explore new boundaries and outside of the box."

"I learned a creative way to introduce the importance and excitement of diversity. I also learned to respect and appreciate the stories of others."

> *"Our education system is certainly oriented around the resume virtues, the skills that you bring to the job market and that contribute to external success. The eulogy virtues are deeper . . . the ones that exist at the core of your being—whether you care, or are kind, brave, honest or faithful, the kind of relationships you formed."*
> —David Brooks, *The Road to Character*

TEACHING TOOL III—
Storytelling

"Storytelling and story-listening opens us to experiencing catharsis, self-discovery, release, gratitude, humility, tolerance, forgiveness, respect, compassion and empathy."
—Kurtz and Ketcham

In this technological age where alienation tends to become the norm, the human connection is even more necessary. What better way to create it than through storytelling? The spoken word is a powerful way to begin the new academic year or new week. Students can learn early that their voice matters and that who they are, where they're from, and what their hopes and dreams are matter. Storytelling develops listening skills, a sense of identity, confidence, and compassion.

Educator Kieran Egan advocates using the story form to teach all subjects to young students. A teacher at Country Hills Elementary in Coral Springs, Florida, is in the process of buying a puppet theater and puppets to "increase students' vocabulary, help them create stories, practice retelling stories, and aid them in connecting with a variety of characters."

STORYTELLING ACTIVITIES

1. Students of different ages, different "multi-intelligences" or abilities and talents can create their own oral or graphic stories with vision boards, storyboards, cartoons, videos, or other form of expression.

2. Students of all ages can produce original animal fables or magical fantasies. This can be a fun exercise to broaden their imagination or a safe way to express a hidden message or lesson based on their own personal and/or interpersonal challenging experiences. Such fables can have a beginning that sets up expectations, a middle that complicates them, and an end that satisfactorily resolves them, as per Aristotle's definition of a story. Two options are:

    a. Each team of students creates its own fable, parable, or folktale via a storyboard with cartoons, videos, mixed media (of photos and illustrations), musical instruments, movement, or song. Each team shares its creation in a circle with other teams for discussion.

    b. Each team of students can search online for different kinds of fables, parables, and folktales; select one and tell the story to other teams. A discussion of the purpose (whether political message or moral) of each story can follow. Teams of elementary students can each select a tale from around the world and tell it through pictures.

3. Storytelling at any grade level can be sparked with imagination, asking students to sit in a circle and use facial expressions and/or hand gestures to enhance it. Elementary teachers can begin with

Teaching Tool III—Storytelling

"Once upon a time" and ask an adjacent student to continue the storyline spontaneously with another sentence, and so on.

4. Middle and high school students might enjoy slam poetry that gives them the power to write and/or perform their own life story. Slam poetry gives students an opportunity to inspire action if they feel strongly about a cause. Individual students or a team of students can tell a story via slam poetry (expressing a personal story and/or struggle usually in an intensely emotional style).

5. Storytelling through different genres of music can be very effective in teaching American History. Teachers, for example, can allude to the story of "Hamilton," the Broadway musical, in hip-hop style, and bring excerpts to the classroom for discussion.

   a. Each team searches online its choice of music genre such as rap, hip-hop, folk or country and selects a favorite style and piece. Each team reflects and discusses the message of the songwriter/singer. The teams can create their own song of a chosen genre and ask each team member to contribute his/her talent or skill. This can result in a team performance.

6. In a Science class, students can research and share stories of inventors. They can, for example discuss Edison's journey on inventing the light bulb with detailed descriptions of his process, that is, his challenges and solutions. Afterwards, students can evaluate, analyze and discuss the meaning of "necessity is the mother of invention" as well as interview contemporary inventors, either orally or in writing, with prepared questions. This activity can be followed by asking teams of students to create their own inventions.

7. Each team of students can interview a family member or a segment of its community and record "oral stories." Storyboards or a video of the interview could be shared at the local historical society or local library.

8. Teams of students can be asked to visualize themselves in a time machine. Where did they land? What period or time of history are they visiting? Depending on the grade and subject being taught,  the people they see can be leaders from American or another country's history, or they can be musicians, artists, inventors, or even their favorite literary characters. As visitors, how are they involved? How are they contributing? Are they reporters who have visited them for interviews? The team members can select the who, what, when, and where as well as their respective involvement. They can also decide as to where and how they could present their stories.

9. With permission, students can be asked to create a time capsule that is to be buried and unearthed in a certain decade in the future. They can include a letter—preferably in permanent ink on acid-free paper, slipped into a protective plastic sleeve—with some social observations of their own era and their hopes for the future. In 2012, Russian workers unearthed a time capsule with a letter from a Soviet youth group from 1979. Some excerpts from the time capsule are "Let your character be courageous. Let your songs be happier. We are certain you will be better than us." What messages do the students wish

Teaching Tool III—Storytelling

to send? What durable artifacts do they wish to create and include to convey the messages? Students need to brainstorm the location for the burial of their time capsule. Once approved and ready, they can invite reporters and all segments of their community to join them in burying their time capsule.

10. Depending on the grade level and needs of students, the teacher can begin a storytelling session with motivating questions or prompts such as:
    - What career do you feel you'd like to pursue? What are you passionate about and how could you share your passion to help benefit yourself and others?
    - What/who do you appreciate and why?
    - For who/what are you grateful and why?
    - When did you have the most fun?
    - When did you feel the proudest of what you said or did?
    - When did you witness someone's most embarrassing moment?
    - What's important to you and why?
    - What or who do you value the most and why?
    - What would you do if you won the lottery?
    - What would you do if you had a magic wand?
    - What would happen if no one knew how to read?
    - What would you change in your school if you were the principal?
    - What would you change in your community if you were the mayor?

    The teacher can then share his/her own story based on his/her own past personal and/or interpersonal experiences.

> *"Thought flows in terms of stories about events,*
> *about people and about intentions and achievements.*
> *The best teachers are the best storytellers.*
> *We learn in the form of stories."*
> —Frank Smith

I began student-testing this storytelling teaching tool with College of Education students by sharing my own story as to how and why I became a teacher. Eager to hear their stories for choosing a career in education, I asked them to reflect on the following prompts:

1. What events in your childhood might have possibly led you on the journey to becoming a teacher?

2. Did a positive or challenging event, person, idea, or decision serve as a trigger or catalyst to influence you to choose a career in teaching?

3. Did an event, person, or idea bring an awareness to a cause about which you're passionate and that you can implement in a lesson plan that would benefit yourself and your students?

4. When and why did you actually decide that you wanted to be an educator?

Teachers-in-Training Tell Their Story:

> "When you started off with your story and had us share (our stories) with our peers, it opened me up to think about what's important in my life."

> "A couple of years ago I got a job as a swimming instructor. The three ideas that triggered this journey toward teaching

Teaching Tool III—Storytelling

were happiness, fun, and rewarding. I always enjoyed going to work because the kids and I had so much fun. When the kids learned the survival skill or stroke, it was really rewarding. I want teaching as my career."

"The childhood event that led me to the path of becoming a teacher was volunteering at a Christian summer camp and working with young children from K–3. Also, a compassionate and humble person helped people reach for their potential, and helped guide adults with differences to become independent and responsible for decision-making."

"I love being around kids, so teaching seemed like the best fit."

"Regarding the path I took to becoming a teacher was seeing my teachers succeed and I wanted to be like them. Also, my aunt was a teacher and I wanted to be like her. She influenced me to be great. I decided to be a teacher in the sixth grade after I had Mr. Melvin as a teacher."

"I made my official decision to teach, in high school, because of my own experiences with disabilities and my love for children."

"I wanted to teach because I was inspired by my feelings and I want to expand students' minds. When I was growing up, I taught friends after school. As I got older, I was a teaching assistant to a teacher that inspired me to become one."

"My 8th grade teacher inspired me to become a teacher. While babysitting, I enjoyed teaching and helping the children."

"Working as an aftercare counselor inspired me to be a teacher."

"I never wanted to be a teacher. After seven years, working with children as an actress and dancer made me love being with children. It took two years after leaving Disney to re-enter FAU and become a teacher."

Connecting Heart-to-Heart Stories

Dr. Susannah Brown, professor of art at Florida Atlantic University and I thought it would be meaningful for teachers-in-training to create a *heart map* collage of stories to describe who they were, their passions, and reasons for becoming a teacher. Their collages resulted in the exhibit, "Connecting Heart-to-Heart Stories."

Students included poems, magazine clippings, and other forms of mixed media in their heart maps. Each map was connected to others within a team of four students, and each team created a team heart map collage that was connected to collages of other teams on a huge window in the College of Education building at FAU (see photo).

Feedback regarding the heart map story project included:

"My poem describes what made me get into education. The pictures around the poem are what I expect in my class."

"The poem I wrote describes what I stand for and what I want to achieve in my personal life and what motivates me to be better."

"My poem is a brief explanation of how I got inspired (to become a teacher); it is a turnaround from a bad experience to a lifelong mission."

Students at all grade levels can create personal and/or team heart map stories.

Validation for the Art of Storytelling

According to Mij Byram, "Storytelling has been around since cavemen told stories of the hunt. Before there was written word, before hieroglyphics, there was the oral story and someone telling what happened to their grandfather."

Many different types of short stories include fable, parable, fairy tales, folktales, myths, and legends. The origins of the fables pre-date the Greeks. *Aesop's Fables*, written by a Greek slave, are popular morality stories designed to highlight both desired and undesirable human behaviors and what to do or what not to do. They also had other purposes: politics (safe expression for criticism without fear of punishment), speeches (supporting one's argument), children's' entertainment, and teaching tool of life lessons at an early age.

Ketcham and Kurtz, authors of *The Spirituality of Imperfection: Storytelling & the Search for Meaning*, have written that "the goal of one's journey through storytelling is to find happiness, joy, peace of mind in our own perfections." They write that in the sharing of each other's stories, one begins the process of self-awareness and the discovery of one's identity or essence. The authors have witnessed how storytelling helps one see him/herself in a new way for the first time.

Tracy Litt-Lester tells us, "Story-listening can be 'selfless listening' (objective) when listening is focused on the speaker. On the other hand, story-listening is 'selfish listening' (subjective) when listening is focused on the agenda and needs of the listener rather than the speaker. Intuitive or powerful listening is the most effective since the listener hears and connects with the real intention/message of the speaker; additionally, the listener hears the words and observes the tone, emotion and energy of what is being said."

Stories evoke images and are more effective when referring to sensory images. We respond with our senses and are changed by the experience. Storytelling breaks down social barriers; it evokes universal feelings and emotions; it gives students a sense of camaraderie as if they were on a team and thus respect each another.

Storytelling can offer a sense of community, a sense of oneness rather than duality, a sense of sharing. Since the mid-1990s, I have invited secondary school students to participate in the *America's Young Heroes* program and contest. Award-winning stories of triumph over adversities through the arts were published in *Teens Are Heroes, Too! Challenges, Choices & Character.* The anthology by, for, and about courageous teens includes stories of personal and interpersonal challenges and resolution with self-respect, respect for others, compassion and caring, fortitude, and an attitude of gratitude.

Teaching Tool III—Storytelling

"Listen! Listen to stories! For what stories do is hold up a mirror so that we can see ourselves. Stories are mirrors of human be-ing, reflecting back our very essence. In a story, we come to know precisely the both/and mixed-up-ed-ness of our very being. In the mirror of another's story, we can discover our tragedy and our comedy—and therefore our very human-ness . . . that lie at the core of the human condition."

—Kurtz & Ketcham

TEACHING TOOL IV—
"What If" Scenarios

"Between stimulus and response, there is space. In that space lies our freedom and our power to choose our response. In our response lies our growth and our happiness."
—Victor Frankl

What if the perpetrators at Columbine High School, Sandy Hook Elementary, Marjory Stoneman Douglas High School, and Santa Fe High School took part in role-playing scenarios or contributed in the "What's Bugging You" activity on page 69 and learned to resolve difficult situations with positive choices? What if they were *taught* to become aware of their character attributes, talents, skills, and potential by using self-assessment tools? What if Eric, Dylan, Adam, Nicholas, and Dimitrios were immersed in daily or weekly teaching tools that could have offered them safe expression for their sadness, anger, or fears? What if they had learned to have hope, self-empowerment, and even respect via these human connection tools? Would Eric and Dylan still have stated on videotape prior to the week of the tragedies, "maybe next week we'll get the respect we deserve?"

American teens are anxious, depressed, and overwhelmed. Anxiety and depression in high school have been on the rise since 2012 after several years of stability. It cuts across all demographics—suburban,

urban, and rural; those who are college bound and those who aren't. Family financial stress can exacerbate these issues.[1]

More than 2 million teens report experiencing depression that impairs their daily function. About 30 percent of girls and 20 percent of boys—totaling 6.3 million teens—have had an anxiety disorder, according to data from the National Institutes of Health.[2]

Janis Whitlock, director of the Cornell Research Program on Self-Injury and Recovery, states, "It's that they're in a cauldron of stimulus they can't get away from or don't know how to get away from." Experts are struggling over how to help them. [3]

What if teens were engaged in deep breathing, mindfulness activities, writing in handmade gratitude journals and positive self-talk exercises, storytelling, self-assessment, as well as volunteering and "What If" scenarios? Could the above-mentioned statistics decrease? Wouldn't it be worth a try?

"WHAT IF" ACTIVITIES

1. Role-Playing

Students in teams of four or five could decide on a controversial issue relevant to teens in their classroom, school, community, or society to resolve via role-playing. Team members can contemplate or reflect on the following prior to role-playing:

---

1. *Time Magazine,* November 7, 2016: "Teen Depression and Anxiety: Why the Kids Are Not Alright" by Susanna Schrobsdorff.
2. Ibid.
3. Ibid.

Teaching Tool IV—"What If" Scenarios

What do you think is the cause of the issue?

If you were in charge, how would you try to improve the situation?

How could you apply your talents, skills, hobbies to resolve the issue?

To whom would you delegate some of the responsibilities and why?

2. Writing an Op-Ed to a Local Newspaper or Social Media Outlet

Students can hypothesize a topic of concern that could have happened to one of them from current events in newspapers, the internet, or television. In teams of three, four, or five, students can brainstorm solutions and compose an op-ed to share with a local newspaper or via social media.

3. Debates or Discussions

   a. Students can debate or discuss thought-provoking questions at the end of each true story in *Teens Are Heroes, Too! Challenges, Choices & Character.*

   b. They can also refer to my blogs on my website www.creatingcurriculum.com for sources of inspiration to debate or discuss.

4. What's Bugging You?

The teacher asks:

   a. Students, in teams of four or five, to write, anonymously, on a piece of paper a challenging personal, interpersonal, school, or societal situation that's bugging them. Each student is asked to place the paper in a bug collection box.

b. One student in the team to pick any piece of paper, randomly, from the bug box, and read it aloud to the team members.

c. Each team to brainstorm a solution to the challenging situation selected.

d. Each team to create a vision board, cartoon, comic strip, or other format that depicts the solution in order to present it to the entire class, the school principal, the superintendent, or the mayor of the town or city.

5. Advice Column

A Q & A advice column can be initiated in a monthly class or school newspaper addressing the different challenging situations, randomly selected by students, in the "What's Bugging You" activity and the corresponding solutions.

Benefits of "What If" Scenarios

1. "What If" scenarios can help teachers encourage students to *identify their unique intelligences and their innate attributes* such as:
    - Self-respect and respect for others
    - Fortitude
    - Compassion and Caring
    - Overcoming obstacles with a positive attitude
    - Gratitude
    - Citizenship

Art by Mark Fitzpatrick

Teaching Tool IV—"What If" Scenarios

2. "What If" scenarios can help students with:
   - Awareness to recognize, understand, and handle their emotions and feelings
   - Self-control
   - Self-trust and self-empowerment, effective decision making, critical thinking, and problem-solving skills in challenging situations; thus, they can choose to transform from a victim into a victor rather than fear criticism, rejection, abandonment, or fear of ego/physical death
   - Empathy for others (even for bullies)
   - Relationship skills
   - Harmony and oneness rather than duality and separateness
   - Respect for each other's diversities, including academic, socio-economic, physical or mental disabilities, ethnic, religious, or racial
   - Embracing their weaknesses as well as their strengths
   - Transforming their pain into "passion with purpose" and sharing the experience for the benefit of themselves and others

3. "What If" scenarios of hypothetical challenging situations would be beneficial in teacher training classes for future teachers to gain more confidence and self-empowerment. With such preparation, teachers would be "role models" to their students by responding more easily with empathetic and compassionate words and actions for a more harmonious class environment.

4. "What If" scenarios in the classroom would also help prepare students to be more empathetic and compassionate as future employers and/or employees in any field.

Dr. Susannah Brown, professor at FAU's College of Education, said that she would use this activity in class "because it can help manage emotions and feelings of frustration."

Feedback from Teachers-in-Training

"I loved both the puppet activity and the 'What's Bugging You?'; I would use them in my classroom, especially the latter. This could be so much help for students who are struggling or maybe some that are arguing. I really love that they could help students with empathy."

"'What If' scenarios would greatly teach students how to constructively solve a problem with others and how to positively change their mindset."

"Yes for 'What If,' which allows students to hash out real life problems and ideas."

Validation of "What If" Scenarios

Edward Guiliano, Ph.D., President of New York Institute of Technology, wrote, "All of the world's biggest challenges demand critical thinking, empathy, cultural literacy and creativity. These skills are cultivated through an education that embraces the humanities." The following are some examples:

- New York Institute of Technology has a frequent photography contest for medical students to help them think more creatively and *build sensitivity*. NYIT also offers a minor in medical humanities to undergrads in order that they can approach medicine and public health from "the human connection."

Teaching Tool IV—"What If" Scenarios

- At the Yale School of Medicine, students must take a trip to a museum to study paintings. This requirement is designed to *improve empathy and observation through sensory experiences.* Practicing observation and enhancing creativity helps strengthen connections to patients, which improves overall patient healthcare.

- The Archives of Internal Medicine published a study that demonstrated that lung cancer patients responded more positively to *empathetic physicians.* Another study observed over 20,000 diabetic patients and found that they had significantly fewer complications when cared for by compassionate physicians.

- In the hi-tech fields, Apple's late CEO, Steve Jobs, stated, "It's technology married with liberal arts, married with the humanities, that yields us the results that make our heart sing."

- The airline industry uses a variation of "What If" scenarios known as a *hiring simulation assessment* in which potential employees role-play for possible employee recruitment and selection. Other employers use such simulation techniques for hiring graduating college students since most don't have work experience. Such a hiring simulation assessment gives students the opportunity to demonstrate their "real potential" in real-life business settings—not just an interview and résumé.

> *"Without the human element, academics is spiritless. With it, there is a bonding and understanding of hope."*
>
> SUSAN SCHALLER, TEACHER OF AMERICAN SIGN LANGUAGE, AUTHOR OF *MAN WITHOUT WORDS*

TEACHING TOOL V—
Volunteering/Mentoring:
Peer-to-Peer in School or Community

> *"Everybody can be great . . . because anybody can serve. You don't have to have a college degree to serve. You don't have to make your subject and verb agree to serve. You only need a heart full of grace; a soul generated by love."*
> —Martin Luther King

VOLUNTEERING/MENTORING ACTIVITIES

How can teachers help students select the type of organization for which they can volunteer?

1. Teachers can help students identify or "discover" their uniqueness, interests, hobbies, and character attributes by implementing teaching tools from this toolkit, such as storytelling and the self & peer assessments questionnaires.

2. Teams of three, four, or five students can select a "classroom cause" for which to volunteer based on issues about which students are

concerned and passionate. These can include the homeless, the elderly, foster children, orphanages, social injustice, illiteracy.

3. Students can select an organization, institution, or people in the community that are in need of volunteers by searching the subject online.

4. Students can select where and for whom they want to volunteer by referring to the stories of the teen volunteers in this teaching tool.

5. Students can also explore and reflect on their passion, purpose,[1] and/or "passion with purpose" when considering where to volunteer by referring to the following questionnaire:[2]

- What is my uniqueness? What are my talents, strengths, hobbies, interests, and/or character attributes? What makes me feel good about myself? What am I passionate about? What do I love to do without necessarily excelling in it?

- With whom or what could I connect and begin to take action[2] in order to fulfill my passion for my betterment and the betterment of another or others? (Family? Enrolling in a class? Joining a club or volunteering with an organization of like-minded people?)

---

1. Viktor Frankl, in *Man's Search for Meaning*, suggested that his depressed, unemployed patient begin to volunteer. Frankl believed that behavior was driven by a subconscious and a conscious need to find meaning and purpose in one's life. By volunteering, Frankl's patient felt like a victor rather than a victim. Victors focus on solutions while victims focus on problems.

2. Many times, one stops from acting upon their passion due to the fear of pain, rejection, or failure. Positive self-talk is one way of overriding these fears as described in Teaching Tool II—Stress Reduction Techniques. That is, one can say, "while I don't like these painful feelings of fear, I can handle them and I'm willing to take the risk and act anyway."

Teaching Tool V—Volunteering/Mentoring

- What positive or negative event(s), person(s), idea(s), or decision(s) has(have) been a trigger or catalyst for change, in my life?
- What issues have or had bothered me at school, work, community, or society about which I could or want to possibly do something today?
- Who has been my role model, past or present, real or fictional (as in a character in a book) and inspired me?
- Which one of my life's experiences (or someone else's) in my childhood or adolescence that might have been painful could I transform into a purpose (to possibly release the pain)?

I discovered my "Passion with Purpose" due to my family's life experiences with genocide in Auschwitz, Bergen Belsen, slave labor camps (Dad) and the Budapest Ghetto (Mom and Dad). As an educator before, during and after the Columbine High School tragedies, I felt that bullying was the foundation for genocide that I wanted to try to prevent.

In my view, bullying was directly associated to genocide since it was initiated by the propaganda and hateful acts of the youth movement in pre-war Germany. The "brown shirts," or Jungvolk, and female counterparts began youth newspapers to overcome the "Jewish monopoly of news"; they also pledged to risk their lives to free Germany from the "shackles...of the enemies of the German race." Members harassed and beat up Jewish teachers and administrators and anyone expressing anti-Nazi opinions.

Did the youth harass and kill innocent people to gain respect? Were they "broken" youngsters who had no meaning in their life or were they just afraid to disobey orders? Sadly, the "brown shirts" chose irresponsible, violent, destructive solutions and overpowered the "white rose" resistance youth movement.

The Columbine perpetrators who were bullied and then became bullies themselves definitely wanted respect; in fact, they stated in a video a week before the tragic shooting: "Maybe next week we'll get the respect we deserve."

How Can Teachers Encourage Volunteerism or Service Learning?

Teachers can create Volunteer Days or Volunteer Months.[3] One or more volunteers can be honored in a classroom setting as Volunteer(s) of the Month. Teachers or students can create the criteria and request a volunteer's "portfolio" that includes:

- A reference letter that expresses the recipient's assessment of how the volunteer made an impact or difference.

- A student's own assessment of the volunteering/mentoring experience and/or benefits received via a poem or essay.

- A student's reflection relevant to his/her volunteering contributions via the arts, such as a video, story- or vision board, photos, Power Point.

Benefits of Volunteering

The Harvard Business School referred to the benefits of volunteering in a study entitled "Feeling Good about Giving: The Benefits

---

3. As an example, I created November as "America's Young Heroes Month" with the approval of the School Board of Palm Beach County. Students submitted essays, poems, art, photos, videos of PSAs, documentaries that highlighted contributions of their heroic peers. Recognition was given to students and teachers of first place winners at district-wide annual awards ceremonies in a designated school.

Teaching Tool V—Volunteering/Mentoring

and Costs of Self-Interested Charitable Behavior." The study indicated that:

- Donating one's time, interests, talents, and skills could build "social circles as well as mental, physical, and spiritual well-being"

- Volunteering could open students up to new experiences and new people

- Helping others could highlight and develop one's talents

- A mentor could discover talents or skills that she/he never thought she/he had

- Mentoring could make one feel needed and therefore boost one's own mood if feeling low

- Volunteering could make one feel more grateful for what one already has rather than what one doesn't have

- Mentoring could be rewarding to see the positive impact of one's volunteering efforts for one or many individuals

At age 19, Kent Keith, a sophomore at Harvard College, said that he "saw a lot of idealistic young people go out into the world to do what they thought was right, good, and true, only to come back a short time later discouraged or embittered because they got negative feedback or nobody appreciated them or they failed to get the results they had hoped for." This led him to write "The Paradoxical Commandments" as part of *The Silent Revolution: Dynamic Leadership in the Student Council*, his first booklet for high school leaders.

Kent gave over 150 speeches in high schools, student leadership workshops, and state student council conventions in eight states. He encouraged students to care about others and to work through the system to achieve change; he also inspired them to persevere rather than give up when faced with difficulties or failures.

Teens' Reasons for Volunteering

"I help by teaching kids how to read because they wouldn't know where to go if their mom and dad told them to go to the store to buy some milk for their cornflakes. I help them solve math problems so they won't get cheated out in the real world when they grow up. I have to play games with them because I think they need a break from all that work they have to do."

"I like volunteering because the kids need my help and I am able to provide that to them; they have a lot of questions and I know they won't ask their mom or dad because I was the same way. I teach them why this is right and why this is wrong. I keep it real with them; otherwise, they wouldn't trust me with their problems, secrets, etc."

"I felt like I was a hero because some of the children (in an elementary school program during the summer months called, 'Streetbeat') didn't know how to read; some couldn't spell and it seemed like they were falling behind for their age and their grade. So I came and helped the children understand how to pronounce words and read. By the end of the summer, the children were reading very well and thanked me for that. I felt honored."

Examples of Teen Volunteers from the America's Young Heroes Contests

In my America's Young Heroes book series, teens have written about their successful experiences as volunteers and/or about those of their peers through their award winning poems or essays:

A seventh grader wrote a poem about her 14-year-old sister who learned how to use sign language and brought smiles to hearing impaired youngsters after school.

Another seventh grader wrote a poem entitled "C.C.C.," which referred to Carolyn's Compassionate Children. Carolyn Rubenstein was 13 years old when she volunteered her time to create an organization with its own website to link critically ill children and children with life challenges to teens in schools via a "pen pal" letter writing program. Carolyn's organization has since expanded to include organizing annual school supply, holiday letters, gift drives and awarding college scholarships.

A Palm Beach County school student wrote about her hero, Micaela, who founded the first Unified Theatre group at age 15 at Conard High School. Micaela wanted to include children of all mental and physical abilities and disabilities, like her beloved cousin, Kelsey, who was unable to walk and talk. Micaela wanted to "teach those who are different to love themselves and to prove they can do anything." Her goal was to have youngsters of all backgrounds come together as equals and put on a musical production of varying decades in American history, organized, written, and directed by students.

"Over 6,000 students with and without disabilities in over sixty schools across the country have performed to almost 10,000 audience members." These role models have had the "ability to unite diverse communities and tell stories that transform the lives of performers and audiences alike."

A ten-year-old girl asked community members and eventually, her state of New Jersey to help ban violent hate videos. This young activist wrote a petition that she presented with over 2,000 signatures to video retailers and local NJ legislators. Thanks to Ashley, the lawmakers sponsored a bill that banned the production and distribution of such videos.

A very young Good Samaritan, who tried to console an elderly couple in a car accident and got run over accidentally by a paramedic, still managed to volunteer. She held seminars, in a wheelchair, for other young paraplegics like herself.

An eleven-year-old girl created an organization with her two older brothers for foster children named Children to Children. "Trying to put herself in the mind of a foster child, she realized that one way to help was give every foster child in America a duffel bag to put their possessions in and a soft little stuffed friend to cuddle when they felt lonely for their families."

An elementary school student pleaded with his grandfather to take him to the store to buy twenty cases of water, forty loaves of bread, and twenty-pound bags of ham. He also asked his grandfather to help him deliver them. This young boy "risked his safety in the

Teaching Tool V—Volunteering/Mentoring

dangerous winds of Hurricane Frances with bad traffic conditions to supply goods for people who didn't have the same luxury."

A fifteen-year-old girl who is not ashamed of the place she lives in, with "broken glass scattered along the roads and the images of the 'thuggish' and 'gang-like' lifestyle," decided to spend all of her yearly savings to buy blankets and provide hot meals for those less fortunate every winter/holiday season...."

A fifteen-year-old girl chose to donate her time:

- Organizing "cleanups" of old playgrounds or streets "to make a neighborhood look and smell cleaner and nicer for young ones to live and play in"
- Visiting different shelters to help out with young children and adolescents

Other teens respectively:

- Read a book to a blind person
- Simply sat and talked through problems with anyone in need
- Shared their story courageously in an American Red Cross program called HIV/AIDS Peer Education; more than 200 high school students trained to talk to middle school students about this sexually transmitted disease and spoke about the importance of making safe, self-respecting decisions about sex
- Created an organic garden outside the school
- Helped disabled parents, sick siblings, or abused children

According to a recent article in the *Sun-Sentinel* newspaper, a sixteen-year-old junior at Boca Raton Community High School and three of her friends initiated "We Dine Together" by distributing fliers, shaking hands with the "quiet kids," and "connecting with the outgoing kids." They've recruited more than sixty students who used to eat alone. They meet once a week to eat pizza, share poetry, talk politics, play games, and plan community service hours.

One of the co-founders stated, "There are so many problems in this world and the only thing that can solve it is relationships."

A psychology professor from Florida Atlantic University validated the need for a club such as this: "During adolescence, kids form a sense of identity based on the social networks they share with their peers as they distance themselves from their parents. A sense of belonging is right up there with food in terms of basic need."

Thanks to these "heroic" teens, they have begun to reverse a trend that began years ago according to volunteer rates from 2003–2005. At that time "Florida ranked near bottom in civic health" due to *decreased* citizen and community involvement, levels of trust, visitation of friends, social ties and social connection, and caring about people, as well as decreased values and respect.

I myself have witnessed the success of peer-to-peer tutoring and mentoring of middle school students using their talents and sense of compassion to help special needs students with homework assignments, preparation for exams, and even playing games with them.

It's amazing as to what one person can achieve alone, or with the help of others, to make a small difference in the life of another while benefiting him/herself at the same time. All student volunteers can experience and develop a sense of responsibility and a "feel-good" feeling, especially those who appear upset, depressed, isolated, and withdrawn.

Teaching Tool V—Volunteering/Mentoring

Volunteering is truly a win-win for those who give of themselves and for those who receive these gifts of selflessness.

> *"Never doubt that a small group of thoughtful, committed, caring people can change the world; indeed, it's the only thing that ever has."*
> —Margaret Mead, Anthropologist

APPENDIX I—
Bullying Prevention Programs, Presentations & Proclamations

Vera Ripp Hirschhorn, M.S., is Founder of America's Young Heroes Educational Outreach. She created the Outreach to help educators implement lesson plans in order to prevent bullying and promote self respect and respect for each other's diversities

BULLYING PREVENTION:
Peer-to-Peer Model for Future Teachers at FAU

I. How can students empower one another to prevent/stop bullying?

1. Research Use of Pop Culture:

    a. Present "self empowerment" songs by celebrities who have been bullied:
    - Lady Gaga ("Born This Way")
    - Rebecca Black, age 14 ("Friday" and "My Moment")
    - Demi Lovato, age 18 ("Skyscraper")
    - Selena Gomez, age 18 ("Who Says")
    - Katy Perry ("Firework")

- Pink ("Raise Your Glass")
- Miranda Cosgrove
- Cody Simpson (CNN), who's urged fans to stop bullying

b. Invite Brett Lowenstern, an American Idol contestant in the top 24 and a senior at Spanish River H.S. Boca Raton to discuss his personal bullying experience and perform his solution, his original lyrics and music to his song, "Bullet Proof Vest"

c. Contact via social networking reps for S.T.A.R. (Show Tolerance and Respect)

Ariel Winter, age 13 of "Modern Family" and August Jones, age 17 of "Two and a Half Men" on skype, or other as well Amber Riley (Glee), rep for Secret's "Mean Stinks" campaign to "take out the trash talk" via facebook.com/meanstinks

d. Discuss anti bullying programs such as Glee which makes it "cool" to rebuke bullying

e. View and discuss teen solutions presented in anti bullying films such as "Hairspray" and "Bully" by Lee Hirsch.

2. Use of award winning art, psas, short stories, essays, plays, music, poetry and boardgames which depict solutions created by, about and for teens; available through America's Young Heroes.

a. Visit www.YouTube.com/use/AmericasYoungHeroes for four art pieces, song, "It Is Now" and four videos/psas: "Be a Friend," "Always Say No to Bullying," and "Meet Me at the Water Fountain…or Else,"

b. Visit blogs@www.creatingcurriculum.com for additional short stories, poems and play

3. Read book(s) that foster self respect and respect for each other's diversities along with 'empowering" activities, art, short stories

Appendix I—Bullying Prevention Programs, Presentations & Proclamations

and poetry by, for and about teens such as "Teens Are Heroes, Too! Challenges, Choices & Character."

II. How can educators empower students to prevent bullying & promote respect for each other's diversities?

1. **Assignments:** Ask students to research historical and contemporary bullies and their domestic/global impact on people and society

   a. Historical:
   - WW II Hitler youth (Brown shirts)
   - How can history repeat itself?
   - What does history teach us so as to prevent the atrocities of the past?

   b. Contemporary:
   - American politicians in Congress
   - political candidates for upcoming elections domestic or global today
   - Ask students for research examples of 'candidates on the campaign trail' with 'respectful personal and social behavior'
   - Ask students for their "solutions" to "disrespectful" candidates, i.e., Role playing, Letter writing to candidates

2. **Activities**

   a. Have any one of you ever been bullied?

   b. "What's Bugging You": At the beginning of each week, ask students to anonymously describe on index cards, "a bugging" experience, ie their "challenges" or "problems" the teacher or a student can select at random an index card and present the challenge or problem written to the class for possible solutions via discussion or role playing.

c. A personal writing exercise in homeroom to help individual students resolve their challenges can be the three paged 'morning papers.'

d. Read literature, such as fairy tales which depict bullying, for example, "The Ugly Ducking," or "The Three Little Pigs" and ask students to write their own fairytales.

e. Write a TV/radio commercial on bullying solutions with an intro such as, "Have you ever been bullied?" or "Were you ever a bully?" or other.

f. Suggest the creation of a 'gratitude' journal with daily entries to help brighten the mood of a student.

g. Give students an opportunity to create videos, artwork and music that depict a bullying experience they had or witnessed which offers practical solutions.

h. Ask students to designate a 'hero,' that is, someone they feel they can go to when bullied or feeling uncomfortable similar to a 'buddy system.' Encourage an activity such as the 'Peer Identification Questionnaire' from *Teens Are Heroes, Too!* to help identify the 'buddy' with whom they would feel comfortable.

i. Refer to interdisciplinary educational resources such as *Teens Are Heroes, Too!* which include inspirational award-winning 'hero' stories by, for and about students; questions to think about and activities to help students focus on their strengths and gifts in order to boost self esteem and self respect.

For example: Mattie Stepanek, age 13, had a rare form of muscular dystrophy: Mattie was taught to celebrate life and play after every storm. He used his talent to write an anthology about life, peace, love and hope, entitled *Heartsongs*.

Appendix I—Bullying Prevention Programs, Presentations & Proclamations

j. Teach civics education to encourage students to be responsible citizens.

For example: "Jay, age 10, witnessed his neighbor's house being robbed by a bully and persuaded his mom to call the police. Jay was asked to look at a police lineup and successfully picked out the robber, who had also stabbed two elderly gentlemen. Jay, whose parents weren't pushing him to do any more, insisted on testifying in court. He felt it was his duty as a citizen of our community to protect others from this criminal by getting him off the streets and behind bars."

k. Help teach the power of gratitude with daily examples from the family and/or classmates:

For example: Rochelle Brown, a new middle school student who "felt alone and isolated among the cheerful chatter" and "shunned from all inner circles" expressed her gratitude in a poem to a classmate who "took in a lonely wanderer; sat next to her and listened with interest; shared jokes and secrets and just became her friend."

3. Refer to quotes for dialogues and discussion such as the ones below:

"I swore never to be silent whenever and wherever human beings endure suffering and humiliation. We must always take sides. Neutrality helps the oppressor; never the victim. Silence encourages the tormentor; never the tormented."
—Elie Wiesel

"If there is no transformation inside of us, all the structural change in the world will have no impact on our institutions."
—Peter Block

4. Teach Self-Empowerment Tools

   a. Assertiveness skills to replace aggressiveness

   b. Use Talent/Skills/Hobbies/Interests Survey from the anthology Teens Are Heroes, Too!

   c. Use My Hero Checklist from same anthology

   d. Use 'My Uniqueness'

   e. Use "My Learning Style Survey; My Feelings"

   f. Refer to Peer Identification Questionnaire in Teens Are Heroes, Too!

4. Present Problem Solving Techniques

   a. Invite young "safe school ambassadors" to discuss definition of bullying, the five common forms of mistreatment ie verbal, emotional, physical,emotional, cyber as well as the possible feelings felt by bullies and victims.

   b. Invite "ambassadors" to present various techniques for resolutions

   - diffusion
   - directing
   - balancing
   - distracting
   - support
   - active listening
   - reasoning

   c. Refer to specific stories, poetry, plays, from America's Young Heroes award winning entries as examples for the above techniques

Appendix I—Bullying Prevention Programs, Presentations & Proclamations

III. How can Educators create a comfortable Environment in Classrooms to be a microcosm of family and society?

1. Visual

   a. Request student produced art, photography/cartoons, posters ... from each student that addresses self respect and respect for each other's diversities

2. Dialogue Training

   a. Students can be encouraged to engage in respectful dialogue ie empathy, openness and equality; that is dialogue that is welcoming, non-judgmental, healing, restorative, repairing.

   Students can be reminded to practice asking themselves before dialoguing:

   "Will my words bring further healing or further anguish?" and "Am I treating others to empower or disempower them?"

   b. Ask students to find such dialogue in the media: newspaper clippings, online, TV personalities, etc.

IV Advocates for Students

1. 2004 Law in Florida to stop bullying: If students use technology to stalk, harass, threaten, intimidate; it's a third-degree felony and student will be arrested without a warrant; School officers, police can prosecute student

2. Jeff's Law includes mandatory counseling for bullies and service to community

   a. Debbie Johnson, mother, teacher at Cape Coral Alternative School, Florida

- Schools need to establish a holistic approach to teaching which addresses the social and emotional components in addition to the academics rather than to the emphasis on testing
- Validate bully's feelings
- Talk to parents of bully and provide them with resources for the entire family
- Punish school districts with loss of their safe school funds to stop cyberbullying
- "We need to be the bodyguards and take responsibility to look out for each other"
- Students can reply to cyberbullies: "Don't send this to me" and students can shut the computer down

3. Safe School Programs

   a. Rick Lewis' Six-Day Plan for the first day of School: respect/compassion/caring

      - Conversations: Listening, Paying Attention to our Intention: What can you do to help someone feel better? To support a classmate who is hurting?

4. Student Ambassadors

Appendix I—Bullying Prevention Programs, Presentations & Proclamations

EMPLOYEE FOCUS

Students and teachers were invited to participate in the "Spirit of Heroes" competition for teaching tolerance and understanding. The invitation was announced in the *Employee Focus,* a newsletter for staff members of the School District of Palm Beach County in the April 12–16, 1999, Volume XV, Number 14 issue.

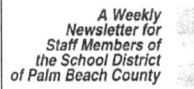

A Weekly Newsletter for Staff Members of the School District of Palm Beach County

Volume XV, Number 14   Week of April 12 - 16, 1999

"Spirit of Heroes" competition

Students in grades 4, 5, 8, 10, and 11 are invited to participate in The Daniel and Judith Ripp "Spirit of Heroes" Award competition. Students are invited to submit an original project, which teaches tolerance and understanding toward people in one or more of the following categories:
1. people of different racial, religious, or ethnic backgrounds
2. people of different physical, mental, or emotional abilities
3. people of different socio-economic backgrounds
4. immigrants
5. people of other nations who have been denied their basic human rights.

All entries must be clearly written and preferably typewritten. The deadline ay 31. Entries should be sent to:
America's Young Heroes
P.O. Box 811332
Boca Raton, FL 33481-0561

I'm Somebody and So Are You!

Proclamation

WHEREAS, the City of Boca Raton, is declaring the month of November 1999 as AMERICA'S YOUNG HEROES MONTH IN BOCA RATON.

WHEREAS, students in the 5th, 7th, 8th and 11th grades in five classrooms of Boca Raton have expressed enthusiasm for the celebration of AMERICA'S YOUNG HEROES MONTH in the school curriculum; and

WHEREAS, "hero" activities and tools such as the "Hero Checklist", the "Talent/Skills/Interests/Hobbies Survey", "I AM A HERO" Photo Display and "Hero Journal" all encourage students to identify WHO they are to help determine HOW to celebrate their uniqueness in serving themselves and others at home, school, community or country; and

WHEREAS, teachers, administrators and school librarians have expressed gratitude and support; and

WHEREAS, several youngsters have already been awarded for their heroic contributions as young heroes who TEACH TOLERANCE & UNDERSTANDING in different categories; and

WHEREAS, it is timely and necessary to help students develop and increase their self esteem in order to be able to cope with challenges at home, school and community.

NOW, THEREFORE, I, Carol G. Hanson, Mayor of the City of Boca Raton, do hereby proclaim the month of November 1999, as

AMERICA'S YOUNG HERO MONTH

in Boca Raton.

Carol G. Hanson
Carol G. Hanson
Mayor

October 13, 1999

1999 America's Young Heroes Month Proclamation, Boca Raton, FL

Appendix I—Bullying Prevention Programs, Presentations & Proclamations

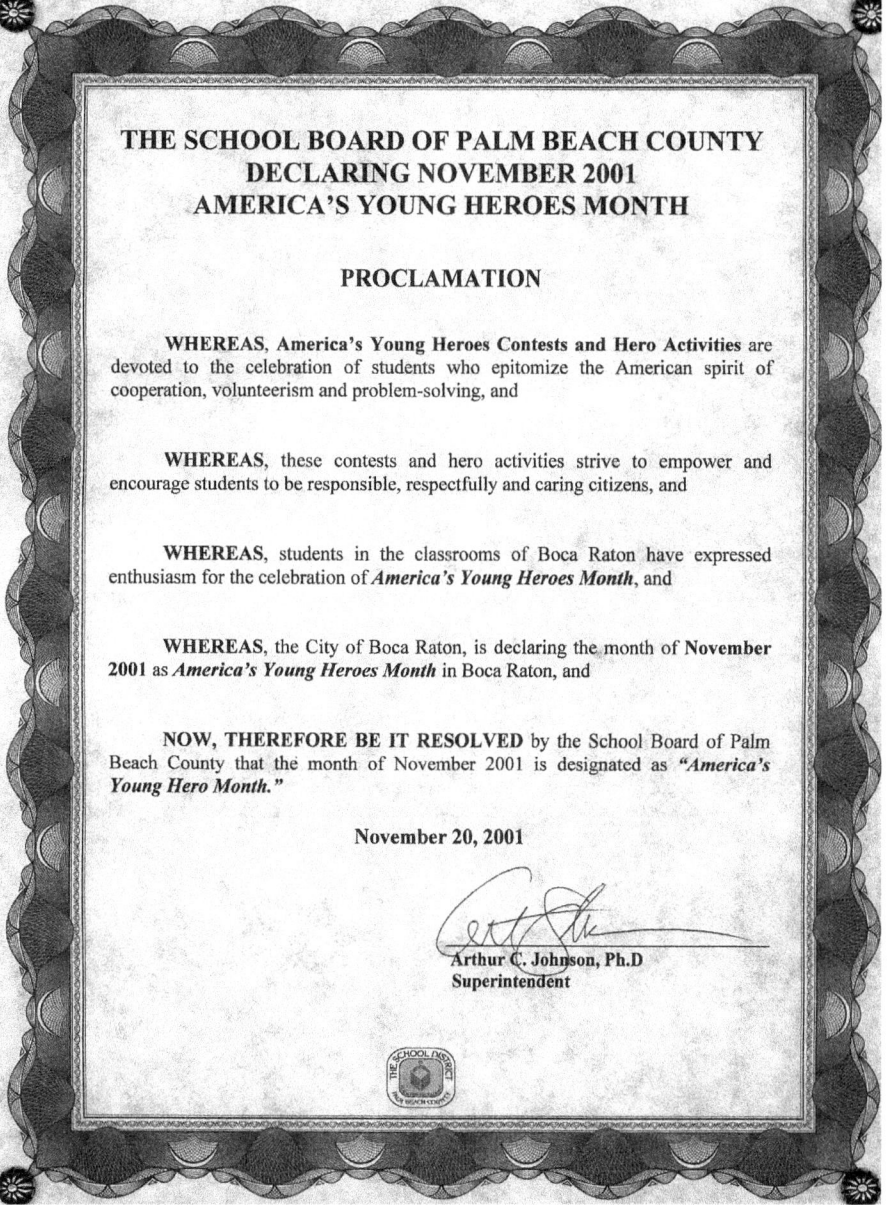

2001 America's Young Heroes Month Proclamation,
School Board of Palm Beach County

I'm Somebody and So Are You!

5th Annual
America's Young Heroes Month in November
To Promote Safe Schools and Safe Environments

TEACHERS AND PRINCIPALS:
GET YOUR STUDENTS INVOLVED IN THE CELEBRATION!

> **STUDENTS IN GRADES 6, 7, 8, 9, 10, 11 & 12:**
> DO YOU KNOW A YOUNG HERO WHO HAS MADE A POSITIVE DIFFERENCE IN SOMEONE'S LIFE? TELL US ABOUT HIM OR HER – THROUGH AN ESSAY, POEM OR ART

The Random House Dictionary defines a **Hero** as: "One who exhibits extraordinary 1.bravery 2.firmness 3.fortitude 4.greatness of soul in any course of action, or in connection with any pursuit, work or enterprise."

Using this definition of a **Hero**, nominate a young hero, age 18 or under from **one** of the following categories:

Category I: (from Florida only)
A friend, classmate, neighbor, family member or even yourself

Category II: (from anywhere in the U.S.)
A young contemporary OR a young historical heroic entrepreneur, inventor, social activist or active citizen

Think of opportunities in which your hero has overcome great odds, improved lives or inspired others at home, school, neighborhood or community

ESSAY	POEM	ARTWORK	MUSIC
Write an essay, typed and double-spaced, no more than 1,000 words. Describe in detail your hero's action(s).	Write a poem, typed and double-spaced, a minimum of 15 lines, maximum of 35 lines. Describe in detail your hero's action(s).	Design a greeting card using any medium, about 5 x 7 in size, that you'd send to a young hero. Use <u>one</u> of the following themes; friendship, compassion & caring, overcoming fears, overcoming challenges with a positive attitude, tolerance, self respect & respect for others, patriotism, volunteerism or responsibility. OR Design a bookmark about 2¼" x 7¼" on America's Young Heroes, using one of the above themes	Write lyrics and a melody for a song (rap, pop or other) about a young hero. Sing it or have others sing it on CD or cassette.

On the back of all entries, write your name, home address, home phone, school, teacher's name, your grade and age

Deadline: Participating Teachers, RSVP Vera Hirschhorn by September 15 at 561 241-1169. All contest entries must be postmarked by October 17, 2003.

Please send entries to:
America's Young Heroes
P.O. Box 811332
Boca Raton, FL 33481-0561

Grand-prize Winners, Finalists, Nominated Heroes & Sponsoring Teachers will be Notified of Awards in November. Possible Publishing of Winning Contest Entries in the America's Young Heroes Journal will be announced.

2003: 5th Annual America's Young Heroes Month Contest

Official Rules and Judging

Essays
Essays should be no more than 1,000 words and should describe a hero based on the definition of a hero outlined in the Contest Rules. Essays will be judged on a 10-point rating scale, with 10 being the highest, 4 points for content; 2 points for creative presentation of ideas; 2 points for organization; 1 point for spelling; 1 point for grammar. On the back of the essay, students must write their name, home phone, home address, school, teacher's name, their grade and age.

Poems
Poems should be no less 15 lines and no more than 35 lines, and should describe a hero based on the definition of a hero outlined in the Contest Rules. Poems will be judged on a 10-point rating scale, with 10 being the highest. 4 points for content; 4 points for creativity; 1 point for spelling; 1 point for grammar. On the back of the poem, students must write their name, home phone, home address, school, teacher's name , their grade and age.

Artwork
Artwork should be submitted on 8½" x 11" paper and may be color or black and white. You may choose to enter one of two categories: Hand-Drawn Artwork or Computer-Generated Artwork.

Hand-Drawn Artwork: Hand-drawn artwork will be judged on a 10-point rating scale, with 10 being the highest. 4 points for creativity; 4 points for artist ability; 2 points for originality. On the back of the artwork, students must write their name, home phone, home address, school, teacher's name, their grade and age.

Computer-Generated Artwork: Computer-Generated artwork will be judged on a 10-point rating scale, with 10 being the highest. 4 points for creativity; 4 points for ability to use the technology in an artistic way; 2 points for originality. On the back of the artwork, students must write their name, home phone, home address, school, teacher's name, their grade and age.

Music
Music will be judged on a 10-point rating scale, with 10 being the highest. 3 points for the lyrical meaning as it relates to the hero theme; 3 points for originality; 3 points for musical talent; 1 point for production. On the back of the CD or Cassette, students must write their name, home phone, home address, school, teacher's name, their grade and age.

Deadline
All materials must be postmarked by October 17, 2003

Thank you to principals, teachers, and sponsors

I'm Somebody and So Are You!

PROCLAMATION

AMERICA'S YOUNG HEROES CONTESTS AND PROGRAM

WHEREAS, teachers and students in the secondary schools of Palm Beach County have participated in the sixth annual Celebration of America's Young Heroes contests and program to build character through literacy; and

WHEREAS, some teachers have included the contests in their lesson plans as writing prompts and preparation for FCAT exams; and

WHEREAS, award winning essays, poetry and artwork have been published in the award winning America's Young Heroes anthology, Book II; and

WHEREAS, a member of the National League of American Pen Women-Boca Raton Chapter purchased and donated copies of the America's Young Heroes Journal-A Celebration to the Gateways Library Program for the Palm Beach Regional Juvenile Detention Center, the Branch's on-going Outreach Project and founded by Kim Hale; and

WHEREAS, contest entries and hero lesson plans will be published in **"Students Are Heroes, Too"** as examples of heroic attributes to solve daily challenges with a positive attitude and positive solutions; and

WHEREAS, student reviews about the contests have been most positive: "It is a great project;" "thanks for inspiring me;" "I now realize that I shouldn't take so much for granted and that I should think about other people and not be selfish;" "I appreciate what other people have to offer;" "(the)....contest has helped me to understand that heroes come in packages both big and small;" "it actually helped me to see that it could be a baby or even me that could be a hero not just the big muscled, super powered people we see on TV;" "this was a lot of fun and I'm so glad I get to be part of the ceremony"; and

WHEREAS, teacher reviews about the contests have been heartwarming: "you are commended for your vision;" "the students benefited greatly from this experience";

NOW, THEREFORE, BE IT RESOLVED that the School Board of Palm Beach County recognizes the America's Young Heroes Contests and Programs.

Done this twentieth day of April, two thousand five, in West Palm Beach, Florida

Arthur C. Johnson, Ph.D., Superintendent   Mr. Tom Lynch, Chair

2005 America's Young Heroes Month Proclamation, Boca Raton, FL

Appendix I—Bullying Prevention Programs, Presentations & Proclamations

---

12TH ANNUAL JURIED CONTEST

CELEBRATION OF AMERICA'S YOUNG HEROES

TO PROMOTE RESPECT AND PREVENT BULLYING

Parents, Teachers, Counselors & School Administrators:
Get Your Students Involved In The "Bullied No More" Contest

Students in Grades 6–12:
Do you know someone who has been bullied and resolved it with positive thoughts and positive action?
Tell us about him or her or even if it was you.
Let Your Voice Be Heard to Help Stop Bullying through the Arts!

What is bullying?

It's a form of verbal, physical or relationship/emotional abuse comprised of repeated hurtful behavior over time that involves a real or perceived imbalance of power. The bully's intention is to humiliate, intimidate, manipulate, frighten, embarrass or isolate his/her target. Cyberbullying is inflicted via phones and computers.

CONTEST RULES:
Submit an original Short Story, Essay, Poem, Song, Artwork, Play, DVD/film or BOARD GAME about bullying which involved you, a classmate, friend, family member or neighbor. Describe in detail how the bullying was resolved with positive thoughts and positive action so that other teens can be inspired. Think about how you can 'give away' your attributes, talents and skills to make a difference in the life of a student who's experienced the mental, emotional and/or physical pain of bullying!

Each entry must include the student's name, address, phone, school, teacher's name, grade, age, photo. Cash prizes will be awarded to the Grand Prize Winner in each category with possible publicity on the America's Young Heroes website, an exhibit, the media or a book.

Music

Write lyrics and a melody for a song (rap, pop, or other) about a bullying experience with your heroic solution(s). Type and double-space lyrics on one side of 8 1/2 x 11 paper. Can be a collaboration between student lyricist and composer. EMAIL MUSIC FILE

Essay, Short Story, Play, Poem

Must be typed and double-spaced. Describe in detail how you or a peer helped you, another or him/herself resolve the bullying experience, or describe how an adult helped you or a peer to resolve the bullying experience with positive thoughts and positive solutions. EMAIL DOC or PAGES FILES

Artwork

Create artwork in any medium; artwork can be computer art, photography, cartoon, a poster about 8 1/2 x 11, a greeting card about 5 x 7 or even a sculpture.
Artwork must depict a bullying experience with positive solutions. Use: acrylic, pen & ink, pastels, or watercolor. EMAIL JPEG FILE JPEG

Board Game

Must include a bullying experience and a practical, original and positive SOLUTION.

Materials must have dice, board game with cards and markers for the board game.

Instructions to play must be very clear.

DVD/ Film

Create a video about bullying with positive solutions; five minutes or less. Select one category: a documentary, short film, animation or television commercial/PSA. EMAIL VIDEO FILE.

Please RSVP by October 15, by sending an email to vera@creatingcurriculum.com
All contest entries must be emailed by November 30 to vera@creatingcurriculum.com
Thank you
America's Young Heroes P.O. Box 811332, Boca Raton, Florida 33481
phone: 561 241 1169

2012 "Bullied No More" Juried Art Contest

Young Heroes Offer Solutions on Bullying, December 2, 2011 (Blog)

Facts:

- Almost 5.7 million youngsters in grades 6-10 experienced some form of bullying according to a National Institutes of Health study

- About one in five teens who have been bullied contemplate suicide

- About 160,000 children skip school each day because of intimidation by peers according to the National Education Association

- Emotional alienation at home can create bullies according to Deborah Prothrowstith, professor of public health at Harvard: "A lot of kids have grief, loss, pain and it's unresolved."

Students, Parents, Teachers, Counselors, Social Workers and People throughout our communities:

What are your Solutions to Empower, Inspire, Encourage & Transform bullies to become benevolent beings and victims to become victors?

Listen to & View the 10th annual America's Young Heroes contest solutions to prevent bullying & promote respect, by, for and about teens.

What If:

One compassionate/caring, classmate, bystander or friend had intervened, as in the award-winning video, "Be a Friend"?

Yasmine wrote in "Speak Out," her award-winning story, that "positive actions make positive reactions; negative actions cause negative reactions," and as sociologist Robert Faris discovered in his recent study, "behavior is contagious."

What If:

The bullied student in another award-winning video, "Meet Me By the Water Fountain …," had the courage to tell an adult such as a teacher, principal, counselor as Allison, a teen poet did and discovered that "one knock on a door opened a new one" for her?

Yasmine, in her story, "Speak Out," told her mom and school dean about being bullied for wearing a hijab, and insisted that they promise to let her take care of the situation herself unless the state of affairs became too big of a problem for her to handle.

And so she sat down with the bullies and explained how they made her feel and why she wears the hijab and how much pride she has for her religion, the hijab and herself. The bullies apologized to her and became her friends and protected her.

What If:

The bullied teen went to the school police officer as suggested in the third award-winning video, "Always Say No to Bullying"?

"A picture is worth a thousand words." And "Music can change the world because it can change people." (Bono)

Check out the award-winning music and art in the video "America's Young Heroes, 10th annual Winners" for more solutions to prevent bullying.

Andrea's song, "It is Now," not only describes her pain as a bullied victim in the first stanza, but also progresses to self-empowerment, as her solution, in the last stanza:

"Moments in time pass by,
We're taking back our lives.
We are standing on our own, and never looking back.
Living with no regrets,
Nothing but happiness
We now know who we are, unveiling the manmade mask.
Years, Days, Minutes, Seconds to overcome
The time has come, and we have won."

Share your suggested solutions; they can make the difference in the life of a child!

U.S. Congressman Ted Deutch has dialogued about bullying prevention before Congress and America's Young Heroes award winners and I are honored to have been included in the May, 2011 Congressional Record.

Let's Dialogue!

Vera Hirschhorn, M.S., Educational Consultant

Founder, America's Young Heroes Educational Outreach

Prevent Bullying & Promote Respect!

Author, *Teens Are Heroes, Too! Challenges, Choices & Character*

vera@creatingcurriculum.com

www.creatingcurriculum.com

Empowering Youth to Discover the "Hero" Within

Appendix I—Bullying Prevention Programs, Presentations & Proclamations

Bullying: Teens' Solutions for Schools, March 9, 2012 (Blog)

Join the America's Young Heroes Project & Become another one of our Model Communities to Prevent Bullying & Promote Respect!

Here is an example of one sector of a community in Florida that got involved in the 11th annual AMERICA'S YOUNG HEROES CONTEST implemented by educators and their students.

View Their Award-Winning Empowering Solutions in Art, Film, Poetry, Essay, and Board Games:

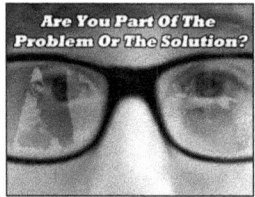

Eyeglasses • Artist: Adam

Got Lips-3F • Artist: Alexis

Camera • Artist: Erick

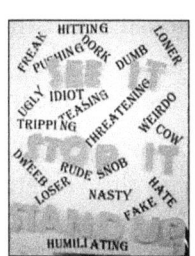

EPrice2 • Artist: Emma

Peace on Earth
Artist: Cheyenne

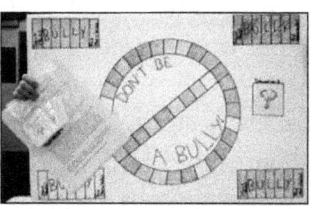

KGruwell2 • Artist: Kaili

GSuper2 • Artist: Grace

Sarah and Alexandra's video shows how a "victim" of bullies chose to become a "victor" through her own self empowerment:

Hailey and Jocelyn's video also depicted how the "victim" decided to become a "victor" when she realized she didn't have to change to fit in and asserted: "I don't need you guys to make me feel popular."

Michelle, Hope and Jessica created their video to show the bully's version of why she 'acts as if' she's a bully; note her initial bully attitude, 'masked' in her body language and compare it to her 'attitude' of low self esteem at the end.

Jack Canfield, educator, founder of "The Foundation for Self Esteem," and co-author of the Chicken Soup book series advises that one of the secrets of success is to start acting like a success before you are one.

In the two stories below, one adult and one student were able to change the attitude of many by emphasizing the strengths rather than the weaknesses of the "victim:"

In Liberty's story, "One Direction," thanks to an anonymous caller who witnessed bullying by four classmates, a principal's solution was to focus on the talents of the bullies and those of their "victim, Harry." After identifying the mutual musical abilities of all, she instructed them to work, prepare and perform together for the

Appendix I—Bullying Prevention Programs, Presentations & Proclamations

upcoming school talent show. Their success resulted in friendship and respect for each other.

In Hannah's poem, a popular high school football player, Malcolm, encouraged the "Garbage girl," a.k.a. the president of the Green Team and lead singer of the "band of misfits" labeled as "Outcasts," to perform at the spring dance. Had it not been for Malcolm's recognition and courageous support of the songwriting and musical talents of his peers, they would have continued to be victimized as "Orc-Dorks," "creepy Goth," and "total nerds" rather than applauded and well-received by the student body.

In Kailen's story, "The Strongest Effect," Meghan, Kenneth's victim, had a choice: to believe Kenneth's hurtful words, like "fat," and "geek," which rendered her insecure and insignificant, or believe her friend's encouraging words and suggested solution. See if she chose an attitude of self defeat or an attitude of gratitude.

Olivia wrote about Johnny's courageous choice to assert himself after being cyberbullied and bullied physically and emotionally for many years: "Stop! Okay? Why are you doing this to me?I have been bullied for most of my life! All I've ever wanted was to live a normal life. I don't like getting beat up; you guys might find it fun, so punch a pillow or something. But stop punching me. I'm done with it! I don't know why you have the need to bully me. What did I ever do to you? Do you want to be the reason I commit suicide? I've actually been thinking about killing myself because of all of you! You would have to live with guilt for the rest of your life! Please stop!"

That whole group didn't know what to say so the main leader said, "Okay Johnny, we'll stop. I'm sorry. I didn't realize how much it hurt you! Friends?" "Yes!" Johnny exclaimed. The bullies and Johnny shook hands and were now close friends. Since the bullies and Johnny were close, everyone in the school started being nicer to him! It's what he has always wanted.

Evalee's story describes the intervention of a friend who told a 'cool teacher' of how Callie was beaten, teased and cyberbullied because of her 'flaming red hair." Read the teacher's decision and the bullies' change of attitude.

Jordan dedicated his video to a 10-year-old girl who committed suicide due to bullying; he believes that a bully should be forced to take anger management classes and, in the most extreme scenarios, be imprisoned.

Haley and Maddison's public service announcement is a warning to all bullies that Bullying can Backfire.

Check out *Teens Are Heroes, Too! Challenges, Choices and Character*, an educational resource implemented in schools by teachers to help inspire students to transform their pain into passion and their tragedies into triumph via award winning art, poetry and essays by, for and about teens.

This anthology has helped identify each student's talents and passions while increasing self esteem, self respect and respect for each others' diversities with activities such as "The Peer Identification Questionnaire," "My Hero Checklist," "Talents/Skills Survey," "Hobbies/Interests Survey," "What's Bugging You?" and "Questions to Think About."

Check out book and/or CD performed and produced by high school students: YouTube Channel/America's Young Heroes (all proceeds from the sale of this and previous books benefit the America's Young Heroes contests and programs)

Appendix I—Bullying Prevention Programs, Presentations & Proclamations

Remember to get involved & Join the America's Young Heroes Project & Become another one of our Model Communities to PREVENT BULLYING & PROMOTE RESPECT

Email: vera@creatingcurriculum.com for details

We're proud to share U.S. Congressman Ted Deutch's congratulatory speech before the 112th Congress • Congressional-2012-221x300

THANK YOU!

America's Young Heroes Educational Outreach
"Empowering Youth to Discover the 'Hero' Within"

APPENDIX II—
Art with Heart Projects by FAU Future Teachers

Journey of Personal & Professional Self-Development, FAU future teachers.

2013 Art Has Character Exhibit flyer in College of Nursing

I'm Somebody and So Are You!

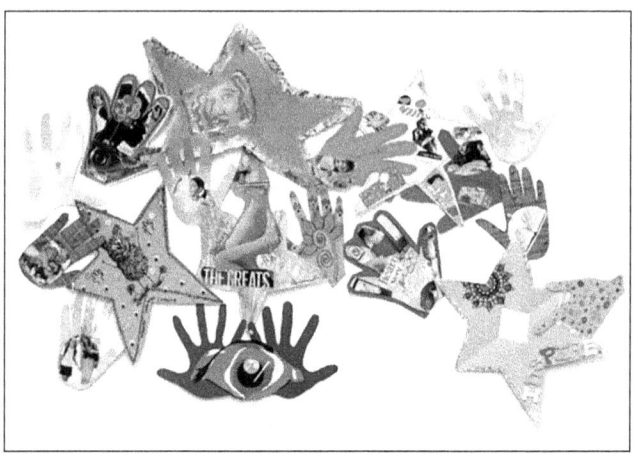

FAU future teachers Self Reflection Collage

2013 Art Has Character Exhibit flyer

Appendix II—Art with Heart Projects by FAU Future Teachers

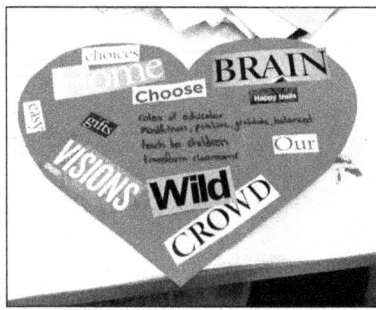
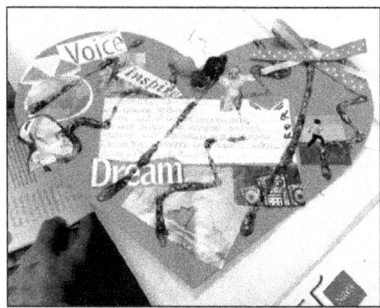

FAU, November 2016: Who Am I? & Connecting Heart to Heart Stories

APPENDIX III—
My Dad's Story [1]

The opposite of love is not hate, it's indifference
The opposite of art is not ugliness, it's indifference.
The opposite of faith is not heresy; it's indifference.
—Elie Wiesel

I was born in Novi Sad, Yugoslavia, on July 24, 1922, to Hinko and Marie Rip, and named Dezider. At a young age, I was educated to be an upholsterer and carpenter. I had my own shop in our home in Novi Sad until 1941. In April, the Nazis occupied my birthplace and I had to do forced labor such as cleaning streets and construction.

Upon my return, my parents felt I should leave for Budapest, Hungary, and stay with cousins, since more and more young Jewish boys were being taken away to working camps. So I lived with relatives and soon got a job and my own apartment. Sometime afterward, my Mom also left Novi Sad for her protection and went to Baya, Hungary, to stay with her cousins.

My Dad remained in Novi Sad. One day, my landlady—whose son was an officer in the military and stationed in Nov Sad—informed me that my father was among those killed during the slaughter from January 21–23rd, 1942, by the Hungarian collaborators. They

---

1. Interview with Garrin Evan Hirschhorn, his grandson, 1991

removed their belongings, including rings and watches, and told them to lie down in the snow-covered, frigid streets, and then murdered them. My dad, the elderly, women and children—whether dead or alive—were all thrown into the icy, frozen, bloody waters of the Danube River. More than 800 Jews and about 500 Serbs were killed in this massacre known as the *Racija,* the Serbian word for raid.[2]

I went to Baya to be with my mom and didn't tell her of my father's death, so as not to worry her. We just told her that he was missing. She left Baya and traveled night and day looking for my dad, and eventually learned of his death. Soon after, we were told that it was safe to return to Novi Sad, where I continued to work in my trade for a few months, during which time I earned enough money to provide my mom with food and other necessities. I tried to calm her during these hard times.

From 1942–1944, I was forced out of my home by the Hungarians and Germans to working camps in different locations. First, I was taken to Coviacha, near Novi Sad, to work the mines, build military bunkers and offices for the Nazis. Then, I was transported, with other Jewish males in a cattle train—without food for one week—to a labor camp at the Hungarian border near Galicia. Here, we were commanded to cut down trees and build wooden roads and bridges. We were then transferred to Tatahago, on a high hill, to work the mines so that the Hungarians and Germans could prevent the Russians from invading.

While a prisoner in slave labor camps, I was wounded in the leg during one crossfire between Germans/Hungarians and the Russians and taken to a military hospital where the doctor insisted on

---

2. Unbeknown to Garrin's grandfather, the Simon Wiesenthal Center identified Sandor Kepiro as a junior police officer, twice found guilty of participating along with fourteen other Hungarian Army and paramilitary police officers in the Novi Sad Massacre of 1942.

Appendix III—My Dad's Story

amputating my leg because of gangrene. The doctor's assistant, who happened to be a "righteous" Croatian from Yugoslavia, pleaded with the doctor to save my leg; in fact, he promised the doctor that he would take special care of it. My leg was in a cast from my toes to my knee for three months. I received crutches from a Hungarian military doctor, and a kind Hungarian priest offered to help me as well.

Soon after, I had to return to the camps where the Hungarian soldiers began beating us—our head, our shoulders and our entire body—with belts, and threatened to kill us because we were Jews. They began to starve us and work us hard. Some of us had to pull horse and buggies with heavy ammunition and build military offices and roads.

We had to sleep in the woods under all weather conditions; our clothes and shoes began to disintegrate to the point that they no longer had soles on them. We were always hungry. We managed to find dirty potatoes and drank green polluted rainwater and developed dysentery. I ran a fever for days and was skin and bones and was so weak that I would fall each time I tried to stand up. *But I never gave up hope of seeing my Mother once again.* Also, God gave me strength.

The Hungarian military only fed us green lettuce cooked in water that was filled with so much sand that our teeth hurt while eating it. We drank muddy, filthy dishwater, which the Hungarians said was coffee. We never saw bread or meat.

We had to continue to put mines in the roads, deeper and deeper. We began to freeze and I remembered my Dad's survival stories when he served in WWI. So, I began to constantly rub my face, hands, feet and all body parts to keep the blood circulating and prevent frostbite. I taught the others to do the same and we managed to survive. Sometimes, the Hungarians would begin shooting at random and kill some of the men. Once, I whispered to the survivors to lie down and pretend they were dead if and when the shooting would begin again.

In 1944, the Hungarian military wanted to remove weak, wounded Jews like me from Hungary and ship us to Germany, but the German soldiers would only permit strong, healthy Jews to go to Germany. One hundred thirteen survived the slave labor camps, including me. We were then sent to the Budapest Ghetto, where 70,000 Jews were imprisoned and where I met your grandmother, who was born in Galanta, Czechoslovakia.

Your grandmother used to remove the yellow Star of David that we all had to wear and sneak out of the Ghetto with her falsified Christian identification papers that her older brother Moric gave her. Under the pretense of friendship with a local Nazi soldier, your grandmother accepted his invitations to dinner. While he paid for the meal, your grandmother would steal bread and quickly place any remaining food into her big black coat's inside pockets. Returning to the Ghetto, she distributed the food to the starving, cold, emaciated, disease- and lice-infested Jewish prisoners. Her other brother, Josef, buried many of the dead. Repeated violent assaults were carried out in the Ghetto, often by members of the Arrow Cross, many of whom were about 15 years of age.

Heavy bombing by the Russians, which killed your grandmother's friend, was most severe when the Russians surrounded Budapest in late December, 1944. We learned later that the SS soldiers of the Reich and Arrow Cross had planned a pogrom in the Ghetto with firing squads. The planned massacre was cancelled thanks to Raoul Wallenberg, who threatened the German SS general that if he didn't stop it, he would personally see to it that he would be charged with murder and genocide by the War Crimes Tribunal. Days later, the Russians entered and liberated it.

Upon liberation by the Russians on January 17 and 18, 1945, I invited your grandmother and a man to return to Novi Sad,

Appendix III—My Dad's Story

Yugoslavia, with me. We traveled three to four weeks by horse and buggy. We stopped at farms to sleep, but couldn't eat anything because of our stomach problems. Upon arriving in Novi Sad to my family's empty home, your grandmother and I got married in the State House and ate food provided by the United Jewish Appeal.

Soon, I was told that my Mom, Marie Berger Ripp, my sister, Irene, and her two little children, Elvira, age 11 and Mira, age 7, were rounded up—along with 1,900 other Jews—in the Novi Sad Synagogue for two weeks and then transported to Auschwitz, where they were gassed in 1944. As for one of my older brothers, Imre, I was told that he was drafted into the Yugoslav Army and had to go to Germany but escaped.[3]

Your grandmother learned that her widowed father and seven of her nine siblings, as well as her niece, Eva, age 6, and nephew, Ervin, age 8, all perished in the genocide known later as the Holocaust.

We decided to have children and our baby Vera, your Mom, was born in 1946; she was named after your great-grandmother, Veronica. A year later, your uncle Hank was born and named after my father, Hinko. Soon I was drafted into Tito's Army and spent six months near Novi Sad and six months in Sarajevo. It was tough under Tito's social communism. There was no freedom; there was strict law and order. Both parents had to work for the government. Your grandmother refused, and so she was constantly harassed and always made up excuses that she was sick, had headaches, and so on.

---

3. Unbeknown to Garrin's grandfather, in 1941, after the invasion of Novi Sad (Ujvidek) by the Hungarians, Imre, his older brother, fled to Budapest. As a member of the youth movement, the Hashomer Hatzir, he took part in the underground activities of the Yugoslav anti-fascist committee; activities included sabotage of military factories, granaries and the like, especially after the *Razzia*, or massacre, in January 1942. He was caught and sent to do forced labor in the Ukraine, where he perished. Imre was posthumously commemorated by the Organization of Partisans, Underground Fighters, and Ghetto Rebels in Tel Aviv, Israel.

Your grandmother never allowed your mom and your uncle to stay in the government daycare centers.

We were all harassed by the authorities. At random, they would stop us in the streets or knock at our door and ask about our purchases. Everything was bought with government stamps—even our food. Each family had allocations. Our family had a vegetable garden and we raised chickens and geese. We also had clothing limitations. In 1948, Tito permitted Jewish survivors to emigrate to Israel.

Between 1948 and 1952, there were six trips by boat for the mass emigration of 4,517 Jews. Our family left on the Radnik (the Worker in Serbian) in 1948, which capsized. Luckily we all survived and arrived in Haifa soon after it received statehood. We were greeted by some Israelis, who took us to Kiryat Yam, near Haifa. Soon after our arrival, I was drafted, and was so mentally, emotionally, and physically exhausted, that I received an exemption.

Life was very hard with bread and milk lines and constant attacks where we lived in a shack near the Lebanese border, today known as Betzet in the Western Galilee in northern Israel, near Nahariya. The government gave us a small farm with chickens and goats. They provided us with eggs and goat milk. In 1952, we left for America, thanks to the sponsorship of my mother's relatives, my older brother, and her older brother, who provided us with employment and housing next to the steel factory where I worked.

Questions to Think About

1. Do you feel that my Dad's story of prejudice, bigotry and hatred in Europe from 1938-1945 is relevant today, in our society, across the country and the world? If so, how? Consider the rise in hate crimes.

    a. Why do you think or feel that people hate or have prejudice? Is it their upbringing? Is it intentional ignorance of a person that is of a different race, religion, ethnicity, or sexuality?

    b. Is it due to a lack of willingness of knowledge and their feeling insignificant? Or do they hate due to fear of change and losing control? Any other reasons? Please share your thoughts.

    c. How can you, as an individual or with others such as classmates, friends or family help lessen different types of hate? Please be specific.

2. Have you or someone you know ever been shamed, humiliated, bullied or discriminated? If so, how did it feel? How did you or the other person respond? Did anyone witness it? If so, did he/she help or just stand by and observe it? Please explain details.

3. Have you ever felt fear of physical pain or death? Or fear of rejection, criticism, or even fear of failure? If so, how did you deal with any one of those fears? Did you choose to accept it or resist it? Please describe.

    a. Do you think that bullies act out violently towards others and even themselves? Consider the rise in school shootings and the rise in teen suicide. Please share your views.

4. Did you know that the intent of the genocide of the Jewish people in Nazi Europe was to completely exterminate them because of

their religion? Are you aware that over one million and a half of Jewish children were killed because of their faith and too young to work? How could you honor them and give them a voice?

   a. Would you be inspired to research and read the stories of these children or the testimonies of the hidden children on the website of Yad Vashem in Israel or the U.S. Raul Wallenberg Holocaust Museum in Washington, D.C.? If so, how could their personal stories be implemented in lesson plans? Have you considered organizing an interview with living hidden children in your classroom? How could they help students?

5. If you had lived during the European genocide of the 1930s and 1940s, what ways do you feel you would have responded? Would you have joined the resistance fighters? Would you have participated in rescue missions? Or any other way? Please explain.

6. What other genocides are you familiar with? Do you feel that "atrocities belong to all of us and that we are responsible for the possibilities that allowed for the perpetrators, collaborators and bystanders to actively participate or look away?" Please explain.

7. In your opinion, what do you feel are the lessons of the genocides of the 20th century? How can they be taught? How can we focus on humanity's weaknesses as well as humanity's strength and human-ness?

APPENDIX IV—
My Stories

America Welcomed Me!

"There was a child went forth every day,
And the first object he look'd upon [and received with
wonder or pity or love or dread], that object he became,
And that object became part of him for the day or a certain
part of the day,
Or for many years or stretching cycles of years."
—WALT WHITMAN

KLM Airlines landed in New York thanks to four family sponsors. On board was a six-year-old girl tightly clutching a little doll. America welcomed this smiling little "miracle" child out of the ashes of war-torn Europe. Gone was Yugoslavia's blood-stained Danube, her embattled communist birthplace, Novi Sad and that of her murdered grandparents, aunts, uncles and little cousins. Gone was death and loss due to crazed, power and hate-driven madmen and women.

Also left behind was the newly created "Promised Land" to which Veritiza's family arrived at the time of this land's statehood, after nearly drowning in the capsized *Radnik*. Absent was their shack near the Lebanese border. Out of sight were the milk and bread lines, baby goats and chicks that nourished their empty bellies. Only a blurred vision of the quarreling, battling children of Abraham remained.

America welcomed Dezider and Yelena—young, resilient, hopeful survivors of the ravages of persecution. Their pain would be masked and buried behind forced smiles forever. At least they were alive! Had it not been for Raul Wallenberg who saved the Budapest Ghetto from being bombed by the Nazis, little Veritza and her younger freckled, redheaded brother, Hinko, would not be here today.

Daddy, how it hurt to feel your anguish and hear your screaming nightmares, jolting me out of a deep sleep every night. How it distressed me to see you disrespected because of your broken English and third grade education. God knows you did your best to raise a family while we lived next door to your uncle's steel factory in Maspeth, Queens where you slaved day and night; Yet, I loved walking there during your night shifts and spending the only quiet and peaceful time I could with you alone. I was so proud of you as they promoted you to night superintendent. You were always there helping the workers and giving them first aid whenever anyone got hurt on the job.

Mommy, how it saddened me that you earned money as a domestic, cleaning the homes of relatives and strangers alike; and you never complained. You were so happy to bring home second-hand toys, dolls, and clothes. I was so proud of you when you became a certified manicurist and stopped working as a domestic.

In Maspeth, having no youngsters with whom I could play after school, I often pretended to be a teacher and take roll call with make-believe students. Perhaps, this was an early sign that I would become an educator one day. I cherished and greatly enjoyed the rare visits from my American born cousins Robert, Norman, Artie, Violet, Mary and Mira, also born in Novi Sad.

I learned English quickly and classmates soon began to invite me to parties.

I even shared a "friendship" heart with Susan Feinstein, one of the popular girls from the 'in crowd.' Imagine that!

I was becoming Americanized! In fact, in 1957, we became legal citizens. Kids automatically became naturalized with their parents, yet, for some reason, I chose to become a citizen, on my own, at age 16.

I am that child that went forth . . .

Becoming a Teacher

Once upon a time there was a six-year-old immigrant child living next to a steel factory where her father worked long, hard hours at night to support her family. There were no youngsters with whom she could play. Somehow, someone had given her a gray-maroon-colored, legal-sized ledger and she pretended to be a teacher. In it, she listed the names of make-believe students and each afternoon, upon returning from school, she would take roll call and ask each "student" to say "present" upon hearing his/her name.

I was that young girl.

As a newly arrived immigrant, I learned English easily, thanks to the tutelage of one of my first inspirational elementary school teachers, Mrs. Adler. Another person who made a difference was Mom, who introduced me to the love of music; she insisted that I learn to play the accordion, which was very popular in Europe, but not with me. I would have much rather preferred dancing lessons. My accordion teacher taught me the merits of the saying, "where there's a will, there's a way," as he repeated often, "Ven she vill, she can."

My mother's influence on my love for music resurfaced when my own children were in elementary school. I, too, insisted that they play an instrument, though I encouraged them to try different instruments. My son eventually chose the guitar, which he still plays, while my daughter chose the flute and played in the school orchestra for many years.

To ensure that they practiced, I learned to be a conductor and created an orchestra with our temple's young musicians. We volunteered to play at nursing homes and at malls during the holidays.

One of my most influential teachers was Dad, who by example taught me to overcome adversities with a positive attitude. He was the most compassionate, caring, loving, and heroic human being I ever met. My father dealt with challenges such as undiagnosed learning disabilities and a fourth grade education with fortitude and strength. Most importantly, he survived and thrived despite his painful emotional and physical experiences of genocide in Europe.

Education: My Passion

Education became my passion and priority because it pained me greatly to witness my dad's frustrations at being bullied by family members and disrespected for his weaknesses rather than respected for his strengths, talents, and skills. I believed that literacy was the solution to all problems and I was determined to excel in school. I realize now that my love and empathy for Dad was my "tipping point" that "triggered" my "passion with purpose."

It wasn't until my senior year at Flushing High School in Queens, New York, that a dear friend encouraged me to go to college because of my gifts for foreign languages, high grades, academic honors, and awards.

And so I became the first member of my entire family to attend college. I enrolled in one of CUNY's top city colleges, Queens College. Tuition was only $24 in addition to books. I earned money by tutoring my favorite subjects, Spanish and French. Russian became my third favorite. The literature, culture, people, and cuisine spoke to me from my middle school years. Having been a Spanish major and

French minor, I accepted the opportunity to study in Granada, Spain, as an exchange student in the Junior Year Abroad program. Since my family couldn't afford the tuition and living expenses, I was able to take a Teacher's Loan, which obligated me to become a teacher.

Upon returning from one of my best personal and student experiences in my life, I registered for the necessary education courses that included student teaching. My internship in a Brooklyn high school was exciting and challenging since some of the scenarios could have been depicted in the movie *Blackboard Jungle* with Sidney Poitier. Upon graduation, I became a proud and eager licensed teacher.

Who would have imagined that the obligation to become an educator for the student loan would pave the way to one of my greatest passions!

Interestingly, none of the education courses, though, prepared me for my first paid teaching position in a New Jersey suburban middle school. I learned that there's always a leader of the pack with whom I had to be "diplomatic" and even empathetic.

An eighth grade female student was the leader who chose to be rebellious and a game player. For example, when asked, "Como está Usted?" she would volunteer with, "I no speaka español." Soon, other students would offer similar variations of Spanglish. What ended the "game" was the one-on-one "human connection." My emphasis on her intelligence, gifts, and skills, as well as her 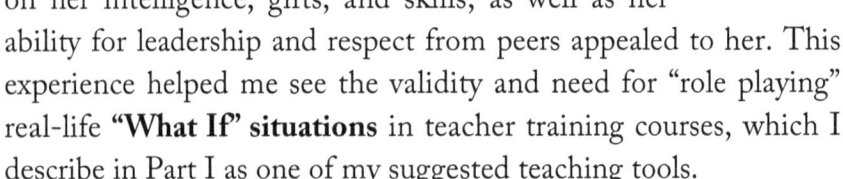 ability for leadership and respect from peers appealed to her. This experience helped me see the validity and need for "role playing" real-life **"What If" situations** in teacher training courses, which I describe in Part I as one of my suggested teaching tools.

Raising My Children & *The Kids' Press*

While raising my children, I taught Spanish and flamenco dancing in Adult Schools at night to make ends meet since my husband had started his own business. Additionally, I created The Language Exchange, an interpreting/translating service for attorneys. I was grateful to interpret at legal depositions in Spanish and Hungarian. I recruited college students for the other requested languages.

During the day, I began to publish *The Kids' Press* for, about, and by students, ages 6–13. I also edited their articles on science, sports, hobbies, music, poetry, movies, and books.

I wanted to give my daughter, son, and all children a positive outlet for creative expression, as I always believed that every child is gifted in some way. My eight-year-old daughter and some of the older students helped me edit and proofread the publication. My daughter grew up to become a professional writer, copyeditor, and proofreader.

The first year of publication, my seven-year-old son sold many copies of *The Kids' Press* at the New Jersey Teachers' Convention in Atlantic City, where I gave workshops on *Students Acting as Professionals*. My son now uses his salesmanship in his own photography business, in addition to his marketing and technology skills.

I received subscriptions and submissions throughout that year and was happy to learn that *The Kids' Press* paved the way for many of the students to become professionals in relevant fields. One youngster, for example, became a professional cartoonist. The only newspaper by and for kids at the time, *The Kids' Press* also led to Children's Creativity Day at a local mall. I invited over 500 young professional elementary students to exhibit, demonstrate, or perform their talents, hobbies, and/or interests in the arts and sciences. This event also made the public aware of existing programs by teachers and schools in basic skills and creativity.

A few years later, I became a permanent substitute elementary and enrichment teacher. In that capacity, I initiated a monthly Great Books program to improve reading and critical thinking skills.

To improve writing skills, I implemented the Young Authors program. Students' stories were "published" in handmade books and sewn by parents who volunteered their time. The school library graciously displayed them in a newly created Young Authors section.

One of the benefits for me, my students, and even my own children was the practice of **stream of consciousness journal writing**, another effective teaching tool that I recommend to all teachers. **Gratitude journaling** also became a part of my life and that of my students.

Teaching for Social Change

While my children were in middle school, I returned to teaching as a full-time "gifted and talented" teacher and used the platform to create curriculum for "social" change. Aware that junk food was sold in schools, at work, and in all public places, I initiated a county-wide, two-day convocation entitled Nutrition Against Disease. I invited speakers like Dr. Lendon Smith, a pediatrician and author of many books such as *Foods for Healthy Kids* and *Improving Your Child's Behavior Chemistry*. Another workshop presenter, Rosalind La Roche, a recovered schizophrenic who founded and authored Earth House, attributed orthomolecular nutrition for freeing her from mental institutions.

Upon hearing the important role of healthy nutrition in healthy kids, teams of students were asked to solve the societal problem of healthcare: "Should the government enforce a law requiring all components of society to practice prevention of diseases?" A minimum of five components such as family, social service agencies, recreational agencies, physicians, schools, insurance companies, restaurants, and businesses had to be selected. They needed to decide to what degree the government should enforce such a law. Their plan had to be original and practical for possible implementation. Solutions were "role played" in **"What If"** scenarios based on the information they acquired from the myriad of speakers.

As a follow-up, my sixth and seventh grade students researched, interviewed, wrote, and acted in their five-minute film, *That's Inedible*, which was aired on television. Once again, students interacted with professionals, including television staff.

Thanks to this convocation and with permission from the Board of Education, I initiated—along with my principal, the Food Services Director, and the PTA—a change in our school's lunch menu. Raisins, nuts, fruit juices, fresh fruits, and veggies replaced high-sugar and processed snacks. I also began workshops for colleagues statewide that addressed the relationship between poor nutrition and depression, teen suicide, and juvenile delinquency.

On a personal note, the convocation inspired me to pursue a master's degree in Human Nutrition and my thesis was entitled, *Pesticides in*

Food Can Be Dangerous to Our Health. And so, I freelanced as an educational and nutritional consultant.

Discovering My "Passions with Purpose"

In Florida, with the arrival of many Russians who had been denied their freedom of religion and their civil rights, I chose to volunteer as an ESOL teacher in the School District of Palm Beach County to help immigrants eventually become naturalized citizens. In gratitude for the successful cataract surgery I had at a very early age, I also volunteered to help a visually impaired elementary school student with his schoolwork. **Volunteering** is another "human connection" teaching tool in my **Toolkit**.

In 1991, my beloved Mom passed away, and in her memory I created a Save Our Earth creative writing competition for elementary school students. Mom loved nature and made all sorts of arrangements with miniature flora and fauna. I was also passionate about protecting our environment.

Three winning **storytellers** whose pieces were relevant to "cleaning up our inner and outer environments" received cash awards on Earth Day and were announced in the newsletter of Florida Atlantic University's Pine Jog Center for Environmental Education. Part I in this book  describes **storytelling** as another "human connection" teaching tool.

After the passing of my dad in 1992, I founded the Judith and Daniel Ripp Spirit of Heroes awards program and invited secondary schools in Palm Beach County, Florida, to demonstrate how they or their peers practiced tolerance and understanding. This program was a memorial tribute to both my parents who had suffered because of the most extreme form of bullying: genocide.

During this time, I also began to research and write stories about *America's Young Heroes* throughout American History. I was most grateful to the teachers in Palm Beach County's secondary schools and the A.D. Henderson Laboratory School at Florida Atlantic University for volunteering their students to test my manuscript. As a result, I created Questions to Think About after each story.

Soon after, I published my first award-winning book of the *America's Young Heroes* series, which profiled courageous youngsters in American history, government, and the military from the 1680s to 1990s.

Preventing Bullying, Promoting Respect, and the America's Young Heroes Program & Books in Florida's Schools

In 1999, I changed the name of my program to the *America's Young Heroes Month* program to initiate "positive contagious behavior." Proclamations were issued by the Mayor of Boca Raton, Florida, the School Board, and the Board of Palm Beach County Commissioners to declare November as America's Young Heroes Month.

That same year, two high school students at Columbine High School in Colorado, Eric Harris and Dylan Klebold, killed students and teachers and then themselves. They had been bullied and stated a week before the school tragedy, "maybe next week we'll get the respect we deserve."

The Columbine school tragedies, followed by a number of other school shootings in the country, inspired me to continue inviting

Appendix IV—My Stories

teachers to participate in the America's Young Heroes program for about fifteen years. Their students were asked to nominate a "heroic" youngster who overcame adversities with positive words and positive choices.

Students' award-winning art, poetry, and essays, as well as thought-provoking questions, were published in the *America's Young Heroes Journal*, thanks to the incredible support and technical assistance I received from Allison Janse at Health Communications, Inc. Additional stories of triumph over adversity by, for, and about students as well as "hero activities" that included **self and peer assessment** were eventually published in the third book, *Teens Are Heroes, Too! Challenges, Choices & Character*.

As a result of the Columbine High School tragedy in Colorado, the mission of the annual America's Young Heroes program and contest emphasized the need to prevent bullying and promote respect. Teachers of all disciplines implemented the program in their lesson plans. Students' solutions to bullying in prose, poetry, digital art, short films, documentaries, and songs appear in Blog I of my website, www.creatingcurriculum.com.

My books in the America's Young Heroes series were created to empower students, emphasize character education, and improve reading and writing literacy. Dr. Richard T. Vacca, an Adolescent Literacy Educator for more than thirty years, wrote in the foreword of *Teens Are Heroes, Too! Challenges, Choices & Character*, that "reading is thinking guided by print and this book, as powerful as it is from a writing perspective, is also a remarkable teaching tool." He added, "Each piece of writing serves as a springboard to reading and more writing. Writing begets reading. Reading begets writing. *Teens Are Heroes, Too!* is a marriage of the two."

What I've Learned

I believed then as I do now, "That the 'human element' is the missing piece to the 'reading puzzle,' especially in our more culturally diverse society where students arrive with culturally different prior-knowledge and insecurities of the unknown." As I wrote in the introduction, "Connecting one on one with each student in helping them identify his/her strength and discover his/her essential attributes or 'humanness' could be considered one of the initial reading strategies."

I discovered many passions throughout my teaching and non-teaching journey. Some were "revealed" to me out of necessity in the same way that "necessity is the mother of invention." During one of the most painful times in my life, I found that the art forms of **journaling**, writing poetry, creating collages, and playing guitar were most healing and a safe, relaxing way to express my feelings.

Nurturing my mind, body, and spirit by having "alone time" at the beach or park, away from the revolving wheels of obligations and activities led me to be more energetic and creative, as did the practice of **deep breathing, mindfulness**, and **positive self-talk.**

This new lifestyle helped me transform my pain into "passions with purpose." It motivated me to create fun and challenging projects for students that utilized my talents, hobbies, and interests as well as theirs.

My family's horrific experiences with genocide due to prejudice, hatred, and bigotry, as well as the Columbine High School tragedy, led me to create the America's Young Heroes Outreach programs and contests. My intention, as an educator, was to emphasize the importance of the character and qualities of students via the arts, for their benefit and the benefit of others.

As a teacher, I realize that educators are provided with excellent opportunities to initiate social change and unbeknownst to me, I became a "social educator." This title was gifted to me in the endorsement of my book *Teens Are Heroes, Too!* by a former superintendent of the School District of Palm Beach County, Florida.

Who would have thought that my interest in my family's legacy (to encourage self-respect and respect for others regardless of religion, race, ethnicity, socio-economic status, academic, mental, emotional, physical abilities, or even sexual orientation) would prompt me to become a social educator or teen advocate?

> *"One looks back with appreciation and gratitude to those teachers who touched our human feelings. The curriculum is so much necessary raw material, but warmth is the vital element for the growing plant and for the soul of the child."*
> —CARL JUNG

My Gratitude List

Special thanks to Dr. Susannah Brown, professor of the arts in the College of Education at Florida Atlantic University, Boca Raton, Florida, and her teachers-in-training for testing my five teaching tools.

Susannah, words can't express my heartfelt appreciation to you for the many years of support you've given me and my educational adventures. Co-partnering and co-teaching with you has been so rewarding and such a joy!

Much appreciation to the administrators, teachers, School Board, Superintendent, and Commissioners of Palm Beach County for their support of my programs, contests, annual award ceremonies, and educational resources in the Palm Beach County schools. Thank you all for the personal and professional rewards I've received since 1999. Please know that I truly treasure the annual proclamations. I am so proud to hang them in my office.

Gratitude to editors Allison Janse and Christine Belleris from Health Communications, Inc., who contributed to all of my awards ceremonies. Allison, you have been such a gift in my life.

Many thanks to all the judges including
Dr. Susannah Brown, professor, Florida Atlantic University, Boca Raton; Kip Miller, professor, Lynn University, Boca Raton; my colleagues from the Boca Raton Branch of the National League of American Pen Women; colleague Myrna Rodkin from Women in the Visual Arts; Judy Fish, sociologist; Dr. Blaise Allen, Palm Beach Poetry Festival; youth librarians and community leaders; *Sun-Sentinel* journalists of South Florida, especially Scott Travis; and former Mayor Carol G. Hanson of Boca Raton. What would all the participating students have done without your help year after year after year!

Much gratitude to all my young heroes and young role models throughout Florida's elementary and secondary schools whose creative solutions initiated awareness of the need to save the environment, teach tolerance and understanding, prevent bullying, and promote self-respect and respect for each other's diversities. Your enthusiasm for participating in the America's Young Heroes contests and programs was contagious.

Great appreciation to provost Dr. Russell and Maricarmen Delhumeau at Palm Beach State College, Boca Raton, for the opportunity to present incoming freshmen with my interactive workshops. It was such a personal reward for me to witness your students' vulnerability in discovering and sharing their uniqueness, strengths, and "passion with purpose," for their betterment and the betterment of others. I am so grateful for the warm welcome I received from everyone.

Heartfelt appreciation to Dr. Suzy Mills, Director of Music Education at the Hayes School of Music, Appalachian State University, Boone, N.C. Dr. Mills, I was so excited with your enthusiastic

My Gratitude List

invitation to consult with your students via Zoom. What a joy to interact with them on developing their own version of a lesson plan, using my teaching tools for their presentation! Thank you so much for your support!

Many thanks to Carol and Gary Rosenberg, The Book Couple, of Boca Raton, for their editorial and design expertise in bringing this book to life. You have both made my publishing experience easier and most joyous!

Special appreciation to Honorable U.S. Congressman Ted Deutch for applauding my anti-bullying program and all the participating students for "their great work and advocacy on behalf of respect and acceptance," and the dedication "to remedying the bullying epidemic facing our schools." Congressman Deutch congratulated the efforts of the contests and the students' "concrete, practical and creative solutions to prevent bullying in America's schools" before the House of Representatives in the 2011 and 2012 Congressional Records. This is an honor I will always cherish and remember.

Many thanks to the TAO community for enriching my personal life.

Heartfelt thanks to Ed Ellis. Ed, you have truly re-ignited my sparks of love and passion for the Spanish language and culture. Muchisimas gracias!

With gratitude to Gail Bluestein, Sheila Firestone, Alexandra Goodwin, Marlene Klotz, Myrna Rodkin, Fran Steinmark, Linda Winters, and my esteemed colleagues of the Florida State and the Boca Raton Branch of the NLAPW. Thank you all for being part of my personal and professional life.

And to Marty, Genene and Garrin, Hank, Maureen, Nikki, Daren and Deanna. You are perfect examples of family that's always there when you need them.

Marty, thanks so much for reviewing one of my most treasured works. I hope you're ready for Part II.

Genene, your editing, your organizing my story with subtitles, and your idea for the subtitle of the book is greatly valued! You never cease to amaze me with your professionalism!

Garrin, your suggestion to simplify the book cover from the very first time you viewed it made a major difference. Your marketing ideas and your continued support and belief in my work has always meant so much to me.

Maureen, I can't thank you enough for being the first to contribute to my scholarship fund for educators in lieu of a birthday gift. It was so meaningful!

What blessings you all are!

About the Author

Reflecting on her life's purpose, award-winning author, and educator of over thirty years, Vera Ripp Hirschhorn found inspiration in her courageous, compassionate parents, heroic survivors of genocide.

As an Educator/Consultant for professors, teachers in training, teachers, principals, guidance counselors, and parents, Ms. Hirschhorn has created programs that reflect her 'passion with purpose' for character education. These are evidenced by her anti-bullying campaign and contests. Award-winning solutions in art, poetry, essays, videos, and songs by Florida's secondary school students can be viewed in her blogs on her website, www.creatingcurriculum.com. The "Art Has Character" and "Heart to Heart" projects by Florida Atlantic University's future teachers can also be seen on this site.

As an award-winning author of *Teens Are Heroes, Too! Challenges, Choices & Character*, and founder of the America's Young Heroes Educational Outreach, Ms. Hirschhorn's mission has been to encourage and empower teachers and students to:

- Tell and listen to each other's stories in order to develop more empathy, compassion, and acceptance for each other's feelings and differences

- Discover and explore their uniqueness, strengths, passions and "passion with purpose" for their benefit and the benefit of others

- Embrace each other's imperfections and perfections

Activities from her books have been implemented at Florida Atlantic University's College of Education for future teachers as well as at Palm Beach State College for incoming freshmen. Excerpts from *Teens Are Heroes, Too! Challenges, Choices & Character* have been included in Dr. Susannah Brown's college textbook, *Teaching Art Integration in the Schools*.

I'm Somebody & So Are You! The Human Connection in Education is Vera's newest educational resource. The toolkit for teaching people skills has been implemented in Dr. Brown's and Dr. Suzy Mills's curriculum for their teachers in training. Dr. Mills, director of Music Education at Appalachian State University, applauded Vera's "approach to integrating art activities with strategies for learning about oneself, diversity, differences, sameness, and challenges of growing up in the cyber-age."

The underlying thread of this handbook, as in all of Vera's previous award-winning educational resources for teachers and/or professional services workshops, is the same: to prevent bullying and promote "self respect and respect for each other's diversities."

Recent honors have included U.S. Congressman Ted Deutch's congratulatory praises recorded in the 112th Congressional Records for her anti-bullying campaign throughout Florida's secondary schools. Vera's poetry and essays have been published in anthologies thanks to the National League of American Pen Women, of which she is a proud member. Poets of the Palm Beaches and the Palm Beach County Art in Public Places have awarded her poems as well.

About the Author

Dear Educators,

If you have implemented any or all of my teaching tools, and they have benefited you and your students, please share your views, reviews, and experiences with your colleagues, Amazon.com, and with me at vera@creatingcurriculum.com.

Also, if you have used my tools as templates and created additional activities, I welcome hearing about them.

For discounts on orders of 10 or more copies, contact America's Young Heroes Publications at 561-241-1169 or 561-302-5709 or vera@creatingcurriculum.com

Yours in Education, Vera Ripp Hirschhorn

www.ingramcontent.com/pod-product-compliance
Lightning Source LLC
Chambersburg PA
CBHW071704040426
42446CB00011B/1901